ON THE COVER
The view from Montezuma Pass road within Coronado
National Monument. Rocks and landforms within the park
resulted from a variety of geologic processes: ancient seas,
cataclysmic volcanic eruptions, tectonic activity and modern
erosion and debris flows.

Arizona Geological Survey photograph by Ann Youberg
(Arizona Geological Survey).

THIS PAGE
Bob Thompson peak rises above the grasslands of Coronado
National Memorial. Morning glories bloom in the
foreground. The peak was created as the area was pulled
apart during the formation of the Basin and Range Province.

National Park Service photograph.

Coronado National Memorial

Geologic Resources Inventory Report

Natural Resource Report NPS/NRSS/GRD/NRR—2011/438

National Park Service
Geologic Resources Division
PO Box 25287
Denver, CO 80225

August 2011

U.S. Department of the Interior
National Park Service
Natural Resource Stewardship and Science
Fort Collins, Colorado

The National Park Service, Natural Resource Stewardship and Science office in Fort Collins, Colorado publishes a range of reports that address natural resource topics of interest and applicability to a broad audience in the National Park Service and others in natural resource management, including scientists, conservation and environmental constituencies, and the public.

The Natural Resource Report Series is used to disseminate high-priority, current natural resource management information with managerial application. The series targets a general, diverse audience, and may contain NPS policy considerations or address sensitive issues of management applicability.

All manuscripts in the series receive the appropriate level of peer review to ensure that the information is scientifically credible, technically accurate, appropriately written for the intended audience, and designed and published in a professional manner. This report received informal peer review by subject-matter experts who were not directly involved in the collection, analysis, or reporting of the data.

Views, statements, findings, conclusions, recommendations, and data in this report do not necessarily reflect views and policies of the National Park Service, U.S. Department of the Interior. Mention of trade names or commercial products does not constitute endorsement or recommendation for use by the U.S. Government.

Printed copies of this report are produced in a limited quantity and they are only available as long as the supply lasts. This report is available from the Geologic Resources Inventory website (http://www.nature.nps.gov/geology/inventory/gre_publications.cfm) and the Natural Resource Publications Management website (http://www.nature.nps.gov/publications/nrpm/).

Please cite this publication as:

Graham, J. 2011. Coronado National Memorial: geologic resources inventory report. Natural Resource Report NPS/NRSS/GRD/NRR—2011/438. National Park Service, Fort Collins, Colorado.

NPS 401/109347, August 2011

Contents

List of Figures

List of Tables

Executive Summary

This report accompanies the digital geologic map data for Coronado National Memorial in Arizona, produced by the Geologic Resources Division in collaboration with its partners. It contains information relevant to resource management and scientific research. This document incorporates preexisting geologic information and does not include new data or additional fieldwork by the Geologic Resources Division.

Coronado National Memorial commemorates the 1540 expedition of Francisco Vasquez de Coronado, the first expedition into the Southwest, and affirms the ties that bind the United States to Mexico and Spain. Located within the Mexican Highland section of the Basin and Range physiographic province, the memorial offers panoramic views of the U.S.–Mexico border and the route believed to have been taken by Coronado through the San Pedro River Valley.

The memorial preserves a magnificent landscape created by dynamic geologic processes acting over the past 300 million years. Principal among these processes was a cataclysmic volcanic eruption in the southern Huachuca Mountains that left a great hole in the ground, called the Montezuma Caldera, and generated landslides, earthquakes, and a complex geology consisting of exceptionally large blocks of broken and shattered strata.

The geology in the memorial provides the foundation for the regional ecosystem, which ranges from grassland in the valleys to a mixed forest of oak, Mexican piñon pine, and alligator juniper at the highest elevations. Geologic processes thus modify the ecosystem and influence a visitors' experience of the memorial. The following geologic issues were been identified as those of highest priority for Coronado National Memorial management during a scoping meeting in 2006:

- Preservation of Coronado Cave. Located within Upper Paleozoic (250 to 300 million years ago) limestone surrounded by Jurassic (146 to 200 million years ago) granite, Coronado Cave contains spectacular cave formations such as stalactites and stalagmites. Dust accumulation and vandalism have severely damaged these formations.
- Water quantity and quality. The Montezuma Canyon watershed drains most of the water resources in Coronado National Memorial into the San Pedro Valley. Groundwater pumped from sediments that fill the valley provides potable water for use at the memorial and for most domestic and industrial uses in the region. Further planned development in the valley may reduce the amount of groundwater available to the park. Increased pumping of groundwater will lower the water table and decrease the amount of water available to ephemeral streams, such as the San Pedro River. Memorial staff cooperate with the Upper San Pedro

Partnership to meet regional water needs and protect the water resources of the San Pedro River. Although definitive water quality data are lacking for the park, surface water samples collected previously from monitoring stations contained heavy–metal concentrations that exceeded the Environmental Protection Agency's criteria for drinking water.

Additional issues relevant to the park include debris flows, abandoned mineral lands, mass wasting (rockfalls), fossil preservation, seismic activity (earthquakes), and safety issues related to undocumented immigrants.

- Debris flows in 2006 and 2008 caused significant damage to the Montezuma Canyon Road, picnic area, pump house, and trail leading to Coronado Cave.
- Although mining is prohibited in Coronado National Memorial, past mining activities have resulted in safety issues that are being addressed by park management.
- Rockfalls and landslides in Carr Canyon may damage roads and trails.
- Invertebrate fossils may exist in the Paleozoic limestone blocks. Interpretation of these fossils and their depositional environments may add to the visitor experience. The invertebrate fossils are very difficult to remove from the rock matrix. They do not currently pose an issue in the park.
- Although rare, earthquakes have been known to occur in southeastern Arizona, including the Coronado National Memorial area. If an earthquake were to occur in Coronado National Memorial, ground-shaking may cause rockslides in the memorial's steep canyons, including Montezuma Canyon. Rockfall debris may damage the park road and visitor center.
- Activities associated with drug smuggling, human trafficking, and the entry of undocumented immigrants into the United States may pose safety issues for visitors and scientists conducting research in the memorial.

Most surface exposures in Coronado National Memorial consist primarily of Jurassic-aged rocks, and most of these are associated with igneous activity that formed the Montezuma Caldera. The complex geology in the memorial and southern Huachuca Mountains involves volcanic rocks, granitic intrusions and related mineralization, and terrestrial and marine sedimentary strata. Beginning approximately 90 million years ago, west–east compression resulting from the collision of tectonic plates formed extensive north–south trending mountain ranges extending from Arizona to Canada. Further geologic complexity was introduced when the crust began pulling apart about 15 to 10 million years ago. Regionally extensive faulting displaced the crust during the development of modern basin-and-range topography in southeastern Arizona.

Rock units in Coronado National Memorial record episodes from the tectonic and depositional history of the last 300 million years. Oceans once covered this semi-arid environment, and after their disappearance, southeastern Arizona became a region of catastrophic volcanic activity. Today, four major biological provinces intersect in the memorial. Although these treasures escaped Coronado and his expedition in 1540, today's memorial preserves this geologic

richness and biological diversity for the enjoyment of approximately 90,000 visitors each year.

A Geologic Map Data summary, Map Unit Properties Table, glossary, and geologic timescale are included in this report. The Geologic Map Data section summarizes geologic map data produced by the Geologic Resources Inventory program for Coronado National Memorial. This report accompanies the previously completed geologic map data (GIS). The Map Unit Properties Table describes characteristics such as erosion resistance, suitability for infrastructure development, potential for geologic hazards, geologic significance, and associated paleontological, cultural, and mineral resources for each mapped geologic unit. The glossary contains explanations of many technical terms used in this report, and the geologic timescale (fig. 16) provides a general reference listing major geologic activity that has occurred over the past 4.6 billion years.

Acknowledgements

The Geologic Resources Inventory (GRI) is one of 12 inventories funded by the National Park Service Inventory and Monitoring Program. The GRI is administered by the Geologic Resources Division of the Natural Resource Stewardship and Science Directorate.

The Geologic Resources Division relies heavily on partnerships with institutions such as the U.S. Geological Survey, Colorado State University, state geologic surveys, local museums, and universities in developing GRI products.

Special thanks to: John Burghardt, NPS Geologic Resources Division Abandoned Mineral Lands coordinator for his information regarding AML features and issues within Coronado National Memorial. Linda Dansby, NPS Intermountain Regional Minerals Coordinator, for her help with updating the closures of abandoned mines in Coronado National Memorial. Philip Reiker, NPS Geologic Resources Division, and Trista Thornberry-Ehrlich, Colorado State University, drafted several of the figures used in the report.

Credits

Author
John Graham (Colorado State University)

Review
Michael Conway (Arizona Geological Survey)
Jason Kenworthy (NPS Geologic Resources Division)

Editing
Jennifer Piehl (Write Science Right)

Digital Geologic Data Production
Stephanie O'Meara (Colorado State University)

Digital Geologic Data Overview Layout Design
Philip Reiker (NPS Geologic Resources Division)

Introduction

The following section briefly describes the National Park Service Geologic Resources Inventory and the regional geologic setting of Coronado National Memorial.

Purpose of the Geologic Resources Inventory

The Geologic Resources Inventory (GRI) is one of 12 inventories funded by the National Park Service (NPS) Inventory and Monitoring Program. The GRI, administered by the Geologic Resources Division of the Natural Resource Stewardship and Science Directorate, is designed to provide and enhance baseline information available to park managers. The GRI team relies heavily on partnerships with institutions such as the U.S. Geological Survey, Colorado State University, state geologic surveys, local museums, and universities in developing GRI products.

The goals of the GRI are to increase understanding of the geologic processes at work in parks and to provide sound geologic information for use in park decision making. Sound park stewardship requires an understanding of the natural resources and their role in the ecosystem. Park ecosystems are fundamentally shaped by geology. The compilation and use of natural resource information by park managers is called for in section 204 of the National Parks Omnibus Management Act of 1998 and in NPS-75, Natural Resources Inventory and Monitoring Guideline.

To realize these goals, the GRI team is systematically conducting a scoping meeting for each of the 270 identified natural area parks and providing a park-specific digital geologic map and geologic report. These products support the stewardship of park resources and are designed for nongeoscientists. Scoping meetings bring together park staff and geologic experts to review available geologic maps and discuss specific geologic issues, features, and processes.

The GRI mapping team converts the geologic maps identified for park use at the scoping meeting into digital geologic data in accordance with their Geographic Information Systems (GIS) Data Model. These digital data sets bring an interactive dimension to traditional paper maps. The digital data sets provide geologic data for use in park GIS and facilitate the incorporation of geologic considerations into a wide range of resource management applications. The newest maps contain interactive help files. This geologic report assists park managers in the use of the map and provides an overview of park geology and geologic resource management issues.

For additional information regarding the content of this report and current GRI contact information please refer to the Geologic Resources Inventory website (http://www.nature.nps.gov/geology/inventory/).

Regional Information

The 1,922.35 ha (4,750.22 ac) of Coronado National Memorial preserve a magnificent landscape created by dynamic geologic processes acting over the past 300 million years (fig. 1). Located in the southern Huachuca Mountains in southeastern Arizona, the memorial offers panoramic views of the U.S.–Mexico border and the San Pedro River Valley (fig. 2). The Coronado National Forest borders the memorial to the north and west, and state and private lands lie to the east.

The Huachuca Mountains are located in the Mexican Highland section of the Basin and Range Province, a geologic province unique to the southwestern United States that extends from southeastern Oregon to northern Mexico (fig. 3). Nearly 40 mountain ranges in the borderland region of southern Arizona and Mexico, including the Huachuca Mountains, are known as "sky islands" because they rise above the desert floor to resemble islands surrounded by a "sea."

Steep mountain slopes and nearly vertical cliffs characterize the northwestern portion of the memorial, and a prominent east–west ridge extends along the northern boundary. Montezuma Peak rises to an elevation of 2,341 m (7,676 ft) and Bob Thompson Peak sits at 2,233 m (7,325 ft). In contrast, the visitor center near the center of the memorial is located at an elevation of 1,594 m (5,230 ft) and Naco, Arizona, which lies east of the memorial on the border with Mexico, has an elevation of 1,405 m (4,610 ft).

The considerable range in elevation within Coronado National Memorial has resulted in a remarkably diverse variety of ecosystems. Grassland habitats in the valleys give way to a mixed forest of oak, Mexican piñon pine, and alligator juniper at higher elevations (Houk 1999). Four major biological provinces converge within the memorial: the Sonoran and Chihuahuan deserts and the Sierra Madre and Southern Rocky Mountains.

The memorial protects the Montezuma Canyon watershed, which drains most water resources in the memorial into the San Pedro River to the east. Numerous canyons dissect the ridge and mountain slopes and drain southward into Montezuma Canyon. Surface flow dissects a broad, gently sloping fan terrace that forms the southeastern part of Coronado National Memorial.

Along with elevation, precipitation plays a key role in shaping the memorial's ecosystems. Average annual precipitation is about 50 cm (20 in) and falls primarily in summer and winter. Summer precipitation falls predominantly as monsoon thunderstorms. Winter brings rain and occasional snow. Riparian zones hug the main drainages, but the minimal quantities of permanent and semi-permanent water in Coronado National Memorial occur in steel water tanks, which collect water during the rainy season, and in a few isolated seeps that result from groundwater flow through fractured bedrock.

Geologic Setting

With the possible exception of the southernmost rock exposures that border Mexico, all of Coronado National Memorial lies within an area known as the Montezuma Caldera. Cataclysmic volcanic eruptions during the Early Jurassic (approximately 200 to 175 million years ago) and in the late Middle and Late Jurassic (approximately 175 to 145 million years ago) formed several calderas in southeastern Arizona, including the Montezuma Caldera, and created a chaotic and unusual geologic arrangement of interwoven sedimentary and igneous rocks (fig. 4) (Tosdal et al. 1989). Subsequent deformation caused by mountain-building processes, igneous intrusions in the Paleogene (65.5 to 23 million years ago), and tectonic extension (pull-apart) in the Neogene (23 to 2.6 million years ago) resulted in an extremely complex geologic setting (Hayes and Raup 1968; Hon et al. 2007).

The violent eruptions that produced the Montezuma Caldera detached shattered blocks of Paleozoic limestone up to 1 km (0.6 mi) in length (Hon et al. 2007). Volcanic tuff, a fine-grained rock formed from volcanic ash, and associated granitic intrusions dominate the rugged topography in the northern part of the memorial. In the southwestern portion of the memorial, the chaotic assemblage of volcanic tuff, lava, limestone, sandstone, and shale is overlain by Jurassic-aged volcaniclastic conglomerate of the widespread Glance Conglomerate (map unit Jg). Clasts in the conglomerate, which covers Montezuma Pass and Coronado Peak, consist of volcanic debris, limestone, and other sedimentary rocks.

Faults in Coronado National Memorial record two major deformation processes that occurred after the creation of the Montezuma Caldera. The older of these episodes, the Laramide Orogeny (mountain-building event), occurred approximately 75 to 35 million years ago during the Late Cretaceous and Paleogene. Reverse and thrust faults (fig. 5) resulting from this period of deformation juxtaposed large blocks of Jurassic sandstone and shale over younger granitic units in the northeastern section of the memorial (Hon et al. 2007).

About 15 million years ago in the Miocene, oblique convergence of tectonic plates along the western margin of North America led to crustal extension and the development of the Basin and Range Province. The crust of the southwestern United States was pulled and stretched until regionally extensive normal faults (fig. 5) formed between uplifted blocks of rock (horsts) and down-dropped blocks that formed structural basins (grabens) (fig. 6). Since their formation, the basins have filled with thousands of meters of sediment eroded from the surrounding mountains.

Two northwest–southeast-trending faults that extend through the memorial resulted from this period of deformation. The faults expose Cretaceous sandstones, siltstones, and mudstones of the Morita Formation (map unit Km), the youngest Mesozoic rock unit in Coronado National Memorial (Hayes and Raup 1968; Hon et al. 2007).

During the Quaternary (2.6 million years ago to present), groundwater percolating through cracks in the limestone dissolved calcite and eventually formed caves, including Coronado Cave, located 1.2 km (0.75 mi) north of the memorial's visitor center. Migrating channel patterns of ephemeral streams left terrace-gravel and alluvial deposits in the southeastern quarter of the memorial. A stable, gently sloping fan terrace dissected by nearly-level ephemeral drainageways extends eastward from the southeastern portion of the memorial into the San Pedro River Valley.

Cultural History

Hunter-gatherers of the Cochise culture lived in southern Arizona from around 8,000 to 300 B.C.E. (Houk 1999). Sparse evidence recovered in the memorial suggests that the Cochise people butchered deer and rabbits and prepared acorns, agaves, and grass seeds along Montezuma Creek and some springs. About 3,000 years ago, the introduction of maize into the region led to the development of farming communities. Apache Indians, a tribal group of Athabaskan-speaking people from northern North America, migrated into the Southwest sometime after 1000 B.C.E.

Europeans first came to this region in 1540 with the Francisco Vazquez de Coronado expedition (fig. 1). Driven by the desire to find the mythical Seven Cities of Cibola (Seven Cities of Gold), Antonio de Mendoza, Viceroy of New Spain (Mexico), planned an expedition led by his close friend Coronado. The expedition followed the San Pedro River through the valley just east of what is now Coronado National Memorial. Although Coronado returned to Mexico in 1542 with shattered dreams of fame and fortune, he brought back a wealth of information about the once-mysterious land and people to the north. His expedition paved the way for later entradas led by Spanish explorers and missionaries (Houk 1999; National Park Service 2007a).

Missions and presidios were established throughout northern New Spain in the 17th century, followed by a few ranches and farms in the 18th and early 19th centuries. Although Mexico won independence from Spain in 1821, control of its northern lands was brief and fraught with strife, especially with Apache Indians. Conflict between settlers throughout the Southwest and Apache Indians (locally, Chiricahua Apache) escalated throughout the 19th century, culminating in a declaration of war on the U.S. military in 1861.

Seeking to expand its territory, the United States went to war with Mexico in 1846. The boundary between the two countries was settled with the 1848 Treaty of Guadalupe Hidalgo and finalized by the 1853 Gadsden Treaty. Thereafter, the U.S. government began erecting stone monuments that clearly and formally delineated the international boundary. Markers 100, 101, and 102 (Marker 1 was located beside the Rio Grande at El Paso) still stand along the southern edge of Coronado National Memorial.

Mining began in the region as early as the 17th century. Spanish prospectors combing the Huachuca Mountains discovered the treasure that had eluded Coronado, albeit not in the form of fabled highways of gold. Their mining efforts are poorly documented, but they did report silver mines in Montezuma Canyon (National Park Service 2006b). Mining began in earnest in 1879 with the development of the Poor Man, Dexter, Annie Mills, Montezuma, Little Maggies, Lookout, and State of Texas mines (Houk 1999).

The State of Texas Mine, which is located within Coronado National Memorial, was one of the longest and most successful operations in the area. Located on the northern side of Montezuma Canyon, assays in the 1890s recorded zinc, lead, copper, silver, and traces of gold ore. In 1928, Tom Sparkes, a mining engineer from Prescott, Arizona, bought a share in the mine, but little activity occurred over the next 15 years. Sparkes died before the State of Texas Mine began full-capacity operations that supplied zinc and lead to the World War II war effort. The mine became the largest zinc mining operation in the Huachuca Mountains during World War II. From 1943 to 1946, the mine produced 1,784 tons of ore that were processed into 150,000 kg (330,000 lb) of zinc (National Park Service 2006b). The memorial was closed to mining by the Mining in Parks Act of September 28, 1976.

Early in the 20th century, the Ratliff and the D'Albini ranching families settled the grasslands at the eastern edge of Coronado National Memorial. William Ratliff established a 65-ha (160-ac) homestead at the mouth of Montezuma Canyon in 1901, and Alex D'Albini claimed 260 ha (640 ac) of land in Montezuma Canyon in 1916. The Ratliff family cemetery is all that remains of these homesteads.

The movement to establish a memorial commemorating the 400th anniversary of Coronado's expedition began in the late 1930s. Grace Sparkes, the daughter of miner Tom Sparkes, inherited the State of Texas mine in 1938. An avid booster for tourism while living in Prescott, Ms. Sparkes moved to Cochise County, and from 1939 to 1952, she applied her experience to the creation of a park commemorating the Coronado expedition (Houk 1999).

In the 1940s, bills were introduced in Congress with the strong backing of the Bisbee Chamber of Commerce. Planners envisioned a park created with land donated by the United States and Mexico. Coronado International Memorial was founded in 1941 with the hope that Mexico would establish a comparable adjoining area (National Park Service 2007a). Although the Mexican government expressed interest in the park, an adjacent memorial was never created.

President Harry Truman established Coronado National Memorial on November 5, 1952, and Grace Sparkes held the post of part-time ranger-historian until her death in 1963. A land trade with the National Forest Service in 1978 extended the northern boundary of the memorial from the Montezuma Canyon Road to the crests of Montezuma and Bob Thompson Peaks.

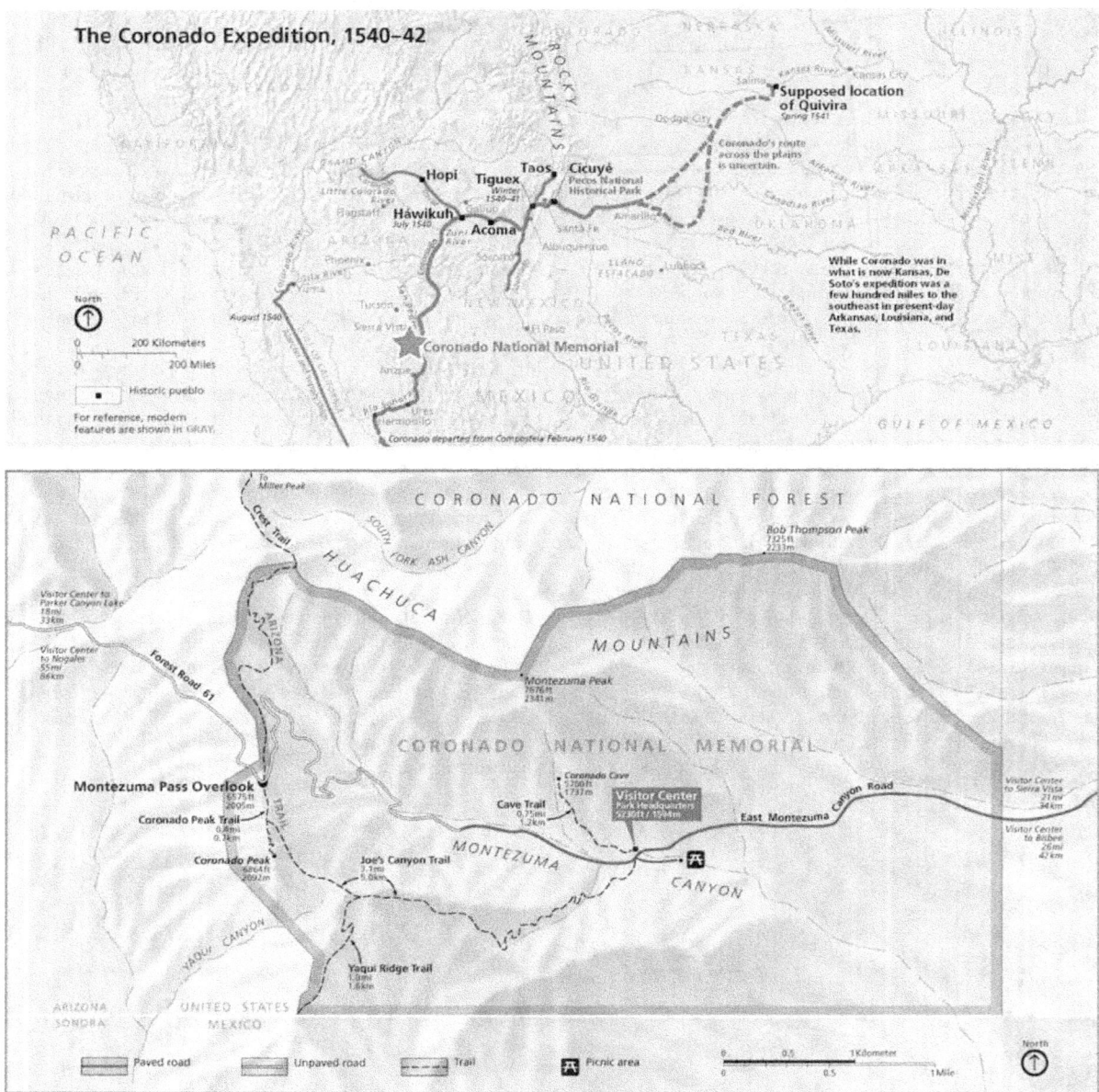

Figure 1. Map of Coronado's Expedition, 1540-1542 and Coronado National Memorial, Arizona. Green star (not to scale) approximates the location of Coronado National Memorial. National Park Service maps.

Figure 2. The view from the Crest Trail, Coronado National Memorial, Arizona. Uplifted along Basin and Range faults, mountains, like the ones in the distance, are called "sky islands" because they appear as islands surrounded by a sea of desert. National Park Service photograph courtesy John Burghardt (NPS Geologic Resources Division).

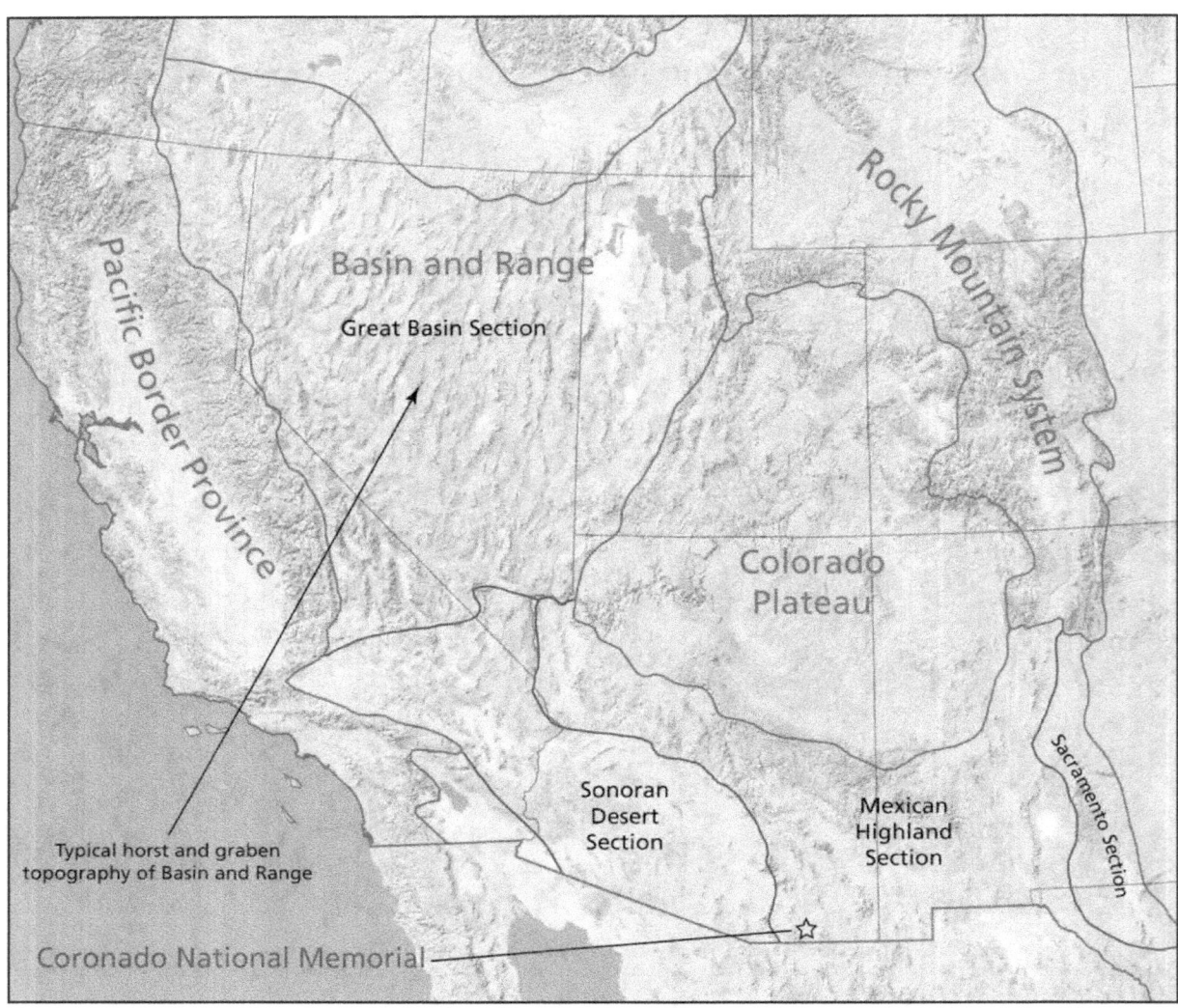

Figure 3. Basin and Range Province of the Western United States. Coronado National Memorial (yellow star) lies within the Mexican Highland portion of the Basin and Range Province. Note the horst (mountain range) and graben (basin) topography characteristic of the province. Compiled by Philip Reiker (NPS Geologic Resources Division) from ESRI Arc Image Service, National Geographic Society TOPO Imagery.

Era*	Period*	Formation/Unit (map unit symbol)		Brief Description
Cenozoic (65.5-today)	Quaternary (2.6 to today)	Colluvium (Qc)		Alluvial fan deposits of gravelly sand at the bases of gentle slopes.
		Talus deposits (Qt)		Chaotic blocks of rock deposited at the base of cliffs.
		Debris-flow deposits (Qd)		Jumbled masses of coarse- to fine-grained sediments deposited from a flowing slurry of rock fragments and water.
		Terrace gravels (Qg units)		Holocene and Pleistocene stream terrace deposits of cobbles, gravel, sand, and silt.
	Neogene (23-2.6)	Regional Unconformity (gap in the stratigraphic succession of rock units)		
	Paleogene (65.5-23)			
Mesozoic 251-65.5	Cretaceous (145-65.5)	Bisbee Group	Morita Formation (Km)	Fine- to medium-grained, well-sorted, quartz sandstone with red to maroon siltstone and shale.
	Jurassic (202-145)		Glance Conglomerate (Jg units)	Fault Contact in Coronado National Memorial
				Volcaniclastic conglomerate, landslide deposits, and basaltic andesite sills and flows.
		Intrusive and volcanic rocks (Jq)		Rhyolite porphyry, irregular dikes, and small stocks of rhyolite porphyry.
		Huachuca granite (Jh units)		Pink to pinkish-gray, medium- to coarse-grained equigranular granite and gray to grayish-pink, coarse, porphyritic granite. Phenocrysts of potassium feldspar.
		Parker Canyon Caldera rhyolite tuff (Jpt)		Red-brown, crystal-rich rhyolite tuff with 20-30% phenocrysts of quartz and potassium feldspar.
		Interbedded sandstone and lithic-rich tuff (Jqlt)		Sandstones, siltstones, conglomerate and thin beds of pink to pinkish-gray, lithic-rich ash-flow tuffs.
		Turkey Canyon Caldera rhyolite tuff (Jrt)		Light tan, crystal-poor rhyolite tuff. Lacks phenocrysts in comparison with Montezuma and Parker Canyon tuffs.
		Montezuma Caldera dacite tuff (Jhl)		Red-brown to green to dark-green crystal-rich dacite tuff with phenocrysts of plagioclase, biotite, and quartz.
		Montezuma Caldera collapse breccias (Jmb units)		Chaotic blocks and shattered masses of pre-caldera rocks enclosed by or interfingering with crystal-rich dacite tuff.
	Triassic (251-202)	Regional Unconformity		
Paleozoic (545 to 251)	Permian (299-251)	Naco Group (Pzl)	Scherrer Formation (Ps)	Quartz sandstone and medium-gray dolomite.
			Epitaph Dolomite (Pe)	Dolomite, limestone, marl, siltstone, and gypsum.
			Colina Limestone (Pc)	Medium- to dark-gray limestone.
			Earp Formation (PPNe)	Pale-red calcareous siltstone and mudstone; some thin-bedded limestone, marl, and chert-pebble conglomerate.
	Pennsylvanian (318-299)		Horquilla Limestone (PPNh)	Medium-light-gray limestone with interbedded pale-red calcareous siltstone and silty limestone.

Ages listed are in millions of years. See the Geologic Timescale (fig. 16) and Map Unit Properties Table for additional information.

Figure 4. General stratigraphic column for Coronado National Memorial. The column illustrates relationships between units within or immediately adjacent to the park boundaries. The five formations of the Naco Group, which are described in the Map Unit Properties Table, are mapped together as "undifferentiated" Naco Group on the enclosed GIS map. The Rainvalley Formation and Concha Limestone of the Naco Group are not mapped in the area of Coronado National Memorial (Hon et al. 2007). Compiled from Hon et al. (2007) and Blakey and Knepp (1989) using U.S. Geological Survey standard timescale colors.

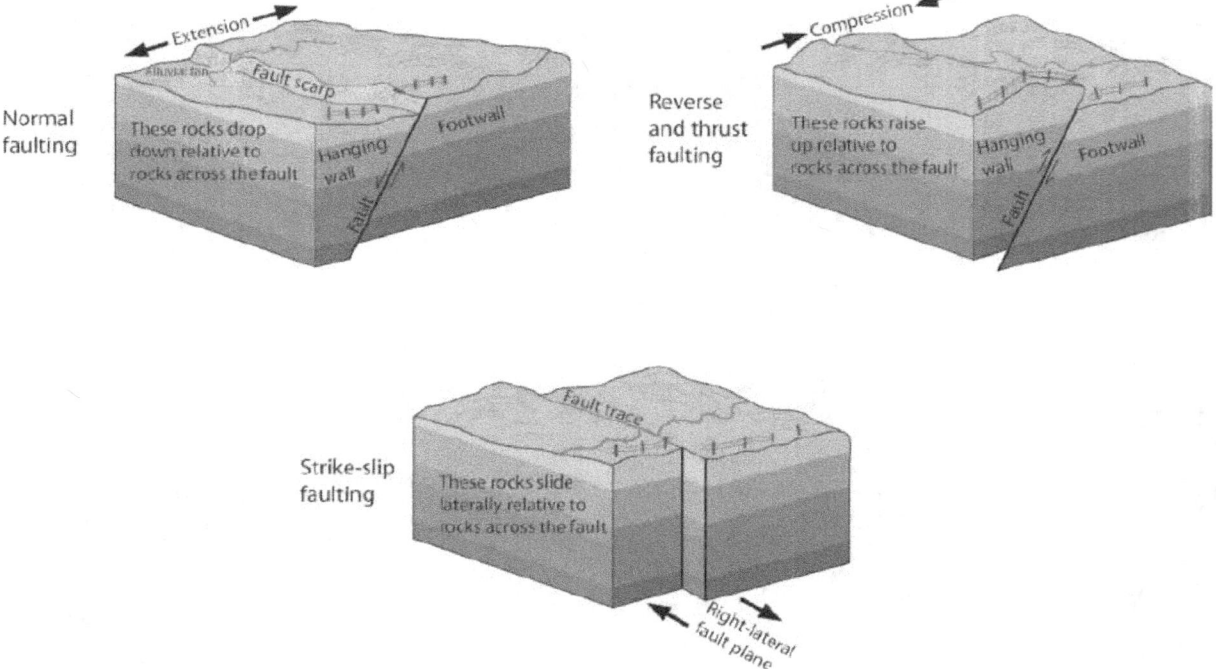

Figure 5. Schematic graphics illustrating different fault types present in southern Arizona. As a way of orientation, if you walked down a fault plane, your feet would be on the "footwall," and the rocks over your head would form the "hanging wall." In a normal fault the hanging wall moves down relative to the footwall. Normal faults result from extension (pulling apart) of the crust. In a reverse fault the hanging wall moves up relative to the foot wall. A thrust fault is similar to a reverse fault only the dip angle of a thrust fault is less than 45°. Reverse faults occur when the crust is compressed. In a strike-slip fault, the relative direction of movement of the opposing plate is lateral. If the movement across the fault is to the right, it is a right-lateral (dextral) fault, as illustrated above. If movement is to the left, it is a left-lateral (sinistral) fault. A strike-slip fault between two plate boundaries is called a transform fault. Graphic by Trista Thornberry-Ehrlich (Colorado State University).

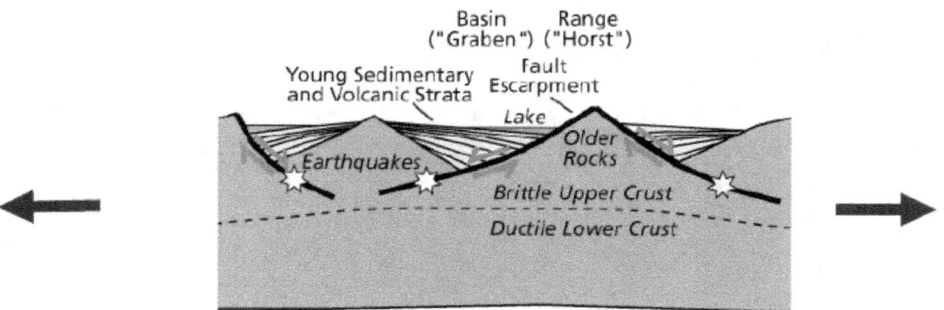

Figure 6. Horst and graben structure of the Basin and Range Province. Extension (black arrows) pulls apart the crust, promoting normal faulting. Horsts are uplifted blocks of rock, and grabens are dropped down relative to the horsts. The grabens fill with sediments eroded from adjacent mountain ranges. In the Coronado National Memorial region, basin-bounding faults separate the Huachuca Mountains from the San Pedro Valley to the east. Tilting of the land surface may result in lakes ponded against the adjacent fault escarpment. Diagram slightly modified from Lillie (2005), courtesy Robert J. Lillie (Oregon State University).

Geologic Issues

The Geologic Resources Division held a Geologic Resources Inventory scoping session for Coronado National Memorial on April 6, 2006, to discuss geologic resources, address the status of geologic mapping, and assess resource management issues and needs. This section synthesizes the scoping results, in particular those issues that may require attention from resource managers. Contact the Geologic Resources Division for technical assistance.

A summary of the geologic issues discussed at the scoping session workshop was completed in 2006 (National Park Service 2006a). The most significant issues discussed during the workshop included:

- preservation of Coronado Cave
- water quantity and quality

Other geologic issues that may involve resource management include debris flows, abandoned mineral lands, mass wasting (rockfalls), fossil preservation, seismic activity (earthquakes), and safety issues associated with undocumented immigrants.

Coronado Cave

Approximately 180 m (600 ft) long and 6 m (20 ft) high, Coronado Cave offers an excellent opportunity to view some spectacular cave features (speleothems). However, the cave and its features have been severely compromised. Cave walls have been defaced by graffiti, dating as early as 1892. Dust blown into the cave by wind and tracked in by visitors covers the cave floor and all surfaces, including the speleothems. The dust limits visibility, may cause respiratory irritation for visitors, and obscures any fossils that may be present on the limestone surface. Although bats may occasionally be observed within the cave, the dust has prevented the cave from serving as a nesting habitat. Permits are not required to visit Coronado Cave (National Park Service 2008a), and vandals have broken and stolen speleothems.

A diverse community of insects, including beetles, millipedes, spiders, and crickets, lives within the cave. These insects are the predominant form of life in the cave and have adapted to dark and sparse environments. Food left by visitors to the cave attracts other insects, such as flies, from the exterior environment; these insects may displace or even replace the native cave insects (National Park Service 2008b).

Coronado Cave has attracted human attention for centuries. Although no archaeological artifacts have been found in the cave, legend claims that the Apache Indians pursued by the U.S. Army used Coronado Cave as a hide-out in the late 1800s. Historical graffiti in the cave dates to 1892. The cave has never been a target of mining activity, nor has it been enlarged for visitor use. U.S. Army personnel from Fort Huachuca have used the trail and the interior of Coronado Cave for training exercises, an activity not sanctioned by park management (Maggi Daly, Visitor Use Assistant, Coronado National Memorial, personal communication, April 6, 2006).

Preservation of Coronado Cave and the other caves in the memorial could be facilitated through a cave inventory. Coronado Cave is not the only cave in the park. Barbara Alberti (formerly at Coronado National Memorial, now superintendent of War in the Pacific National Historical Park, personal communication, April 28, 2006) counted nine cave/karst features in the memorial, and additional smaller karst features are also present in the park. Six of the nine caves have been located using a global positioning system (GPS; Kelly LaCroix, graduate student, University of Arizona, personal communication, April 6, 2006), but none had been explored at the time of the scoping meeting (National Park Service 2006a).

Once the caves in Coronado National Memorial have been documented, an inventory and cave–management plan are recommended additions to park management. A cave inventory could identify vital signs that should be monitored to facilitate the conservation, restoration, and protection of resources in Coronado Cave and the other caves in the memorial.

Toomey (2009) has described inventory and monitoring methods using vital signs in caves and karst features. Vital signs are measurable parameters of the overall condition of the cave system, including: 1) cave meteorology (microclimate, air composition), 2) airborne sedimentation (dust, lint), 3) direct visitor impacts (e.g., breakage of cave formations, trail use in caves, graffiti, cave lighting), 4) presence of permanent or seasonal ice, 5) cave-drip and pool-water (locations, rate, volume, water chemistry, microbiology, temperature), 6) microbiology, 7) stability-breakdown, rockfall and partings, 8) mineral growth (speleothems: stalagmites, stalactites), 9) surface expressions and processes (e.g., karst processes linking surface to cave through springs, sinkholes, cracks), 10) regional groundwater levels and quantity, and 11) fluvial processes (underground streams and rivers) (Toomey 2009).

Not all vital signs apply to every cave, but an inventory should identify the significant vital signs for each case or region. Inventories should catalog not only geological resources, but also biological (e.g., bats, other vertebrates, invertebrates, microbiology), cultural (archaeological, historical), and paleontological resources (Toomey 2009). Carlsbad Caverns National Park has recently developed a cave-management plan (Carlsbad Caverns National Park 2006) that may serve as a reference for resource managers interested in developing monitoring protocols for the cave and karst resources in Coronado National Memorial.

Water Quantity and Quality

Projections of future climate change suggest that water supplies in the Southwest will become increasingly scarce (Karl et al. 2009). Landscapes and ecosystems will be transformed by increasing temperatures, drought, wildfires, and invasive species. The non-native buffelgrass (*Pennisetum ciliare*), for example, has become a major threat to the Sonoran Desert ecosystem. Introduced from Africa for cattle forage, buffelgrass claims soil moisture needed by larger plants to survive, and because it grows densely, it crowds out native plants of similar size (Michael Conway, Geologist, Arizona Geological Survey, written communication, February 27, 2011). Buffelgrass is drought-tolerant, so it can remain dense and even spread during dry years. Removal of buffelgrass is labor intensive, often requiring the use of shovels and crowbars to pull larger plants. At Saguaro National Park near Tucson, volunteers log hundreds of hours pulling buffelgrass. Seeds from the invasive plant can remain dormant for years, so once the plants are removed, the area must be periodically checked for new seedlings.

Increased groundwater pumping will lower water tables and rising temperatures will reduce river flows. Many of these streams, such as the San Pedro River, are ephemeral streams that flow briefly in response to local precipitation. Ephemeral streams lose water as it flows downstream. Because the water table is below the bottom of the stream, water in the stream seeps into the ground. In the arid Southwest, this soil moisture may be captured by plants, may interact with minerals in the soil to form hard layers, such as caliche, or may eventually reach the water table. As water tables drop, however, less of this water recharges groundwater systems.

Paradoxically, flooding may also increase due to increased precipitation from more intense storm events, including more rain-on-snow events causing rapid runoff in areas where increased drought conditions and fires have reduced vegetation cover (Karl et al. 2009). By 2010, Arizona had experienced a decade-long drought leading to reduced water levels in lakes and reservoirs. Additional information about the potential effects of global climate change in Arizona is available on the website of the Arizona Climate Change Advisory Group (http://www.azclimatechange.gov/, accessed April 28, 2010).

Coronado National Memorial encompasses most of the Montezuma Canyon watershed, which drains southeast into the San Pedro River. Supporting only ephemeral flow, the San Pedro River is one of the last undammed large rivers in the Southwest and one of only two rivers that flows north from Mexico into the United States.

Through membership in the Upper San Pedro Partnership, Coronado National Memorial staff work with representatives of other agencies and groups to meet regional water needs and to protect San Pedro River resources.

Located in Fort Collins, Colorado, the Water Resources Division (WRD) of the National Park Service addresses water issues in the parks (http://www.nature.nps.gov/water/). The following information summarizes some of the water issues discussed at the scoping workshop, but resource managers should contact the WRD with additional concerns.

Groundwater

In the Upper San Pedro basin, groundwater flows in two major sediment units: 1) alluvial basin-fill sediments in the valley and 2) streambed alluvium forming the channel and floodplain of the San Pedro River (Arizona Department of Water Resources 2009). Researchers with the Arizona Geological Survey recently mapped the Holocene channel and floodplain alluvium and delineated subflow zones in the San Pedro River watershed (Cook et al. 2009). Basin-fill sediments up to 460 m (1,500 ft) in thickness constitute the primary regional aquifer (water-bearing unit), within which water wells yield 380 to 11,000 L/min (100 to 2,800 gal/min) of water.

Groundwater flows into the valley from higher elevations in the mountains and then travels northwest along the riverbed. The bedrock in the mountains yields groundwater only where sufficiently faulted and fractured. Most mountain springs are small, and measured discharges vary greatly. Water wells in the regional basin-fill aquifer supply most industrial and domestic/public uses in the valley.

Potable water supplies for Coronado National Memorial depend on the quality and quantity of groundwater, which may become a significant issue in the future. Real estate developers have purchased a ranch located southwest of Coronado National Memorial, and plan to construct 400 homes on that land (Maggi Daly, Visitor Use Assistant, Coronado National Memorial, personal communication April 6, 2006). Groundwater levels may drop due to drought conditions and-/or increased demand created by this development.

Surface Water

Surface water has been sporadically monitored at Coronado National Memorial (1965, 1993, 2003). The 1965 and 1993 data were summarized in a 2000 WRD report (Water Resources Division 2000), which states that surface-water samples collected in 1965 from Brown Allotment Spring on Bob Thompson Peak (water quality monitoring station CORO0003), Tunnel Mine Spring near Montezuma Pass (CORO0008), and Yaqui Spring south of Coronado Peak (CORO0009) yielded pH values of 7.9, 8.0, and 7.6, respectively. No contaminants were detected in the samples, although they were not tested for heavy metals.

In 1993, heavy-metal concentrations were measured in surface-water samples collected from four sites (CORO0004, CORO0005, CORO0006, CORO0007) associated with abandoned Copper Mine No. 93-025, located approximately 0.6 km (1 mi) northwest of park headquarters. Heavy-metal concentrations exceeding the U.S. Environmental Protection Agency's (EPA) Maximum Contaminant Levels for drinking water or acute freshwater were recorded at three of the sites (Table 1; refer to (http://water.epa.gov/drink/contaminants/index.cfm for current standards). The WRD concluded that the limited sampling from 1965 and 1993 did not provide sufficient water-quality data to make definitive statements regarding surface-water quality within Coronado National Memorial (Water Resources Division 2000).

In 2003 and 2004, the U.S. Geological Survey Arizona Water Science Center collected water samples from seeps, springs, wells, mine adits, and streams in 9 park units in southern and central Arizona and west-central New Mexico (Brown 2005). Eight sites were sampled in Coronado National Memorial. High concentrations of heavy metals were found at Blue Waterfall seep, located below an unnamed mine in the memorial, and concentrations of dissolved uranium that exceeded the MCL of 10 micrograms per liter for drinking water were recorded from 7 sites, including Blue Waterfall seep (Table 1). The highest concentrations of dissolved uranium occurred at the State of Texas Mine, ranging from 113 to 122 micrograms per liter (Brown 2005).

In addition to high heavy-metal concentrations related to mining activity, water at Blue Waterfall also exhibits naturally low pH levels (Charles Ferguson, Arizona Geological Survey, and Floyd Gray, U.S. Geological Survey, personal communication, April 2006). Located in a rugged off-trail area of the memorial, the waterfall does not present a management issue at this time.

Mass Wasting

Mass wasting refers to any dislodgement and downslope movement of rock and/or soil material. Mass wasting can be fast, as with the debris flow and rockfall within Coronado National Memorial, or slow as with soil creep and slumping.

Debris Flows

Flow types categorized as debris flows range along a continuum from sediment-rich slurries to water flows (floods). Sediment-rich slurries transport clay, silt, and occasionally sand in suspended loads and gravel and boulders in bedloads. Triggered by different types of slope failure, debris flows pose significant geologic hazards to the mountains and canyons of Arizona (Wohl and Pearthree 1991; Pearthree and Youberg 2006; Youberg et al. 2008). They have caused significant damage to Coronado National Memorial, as detailed below.

The episodic nature of debris flows suggests a relationship between rates of slope weathering and subsequent erosion, which, in turn, are controlled by degree of vegetation cover and fire events (Wohl and Pearthree 1991). Research has indicated that surface runoff in the steep drainage basins of the Huachuca Mountains has increased after fires denuded the hillslopes of their vegetative cover. However, not every fire has been associated with a debris flow, and such geologic hazards can also occur in the absence of fire.

Rare, extreme precipitation events may trigger slope failures that result in debris flows. Mean annual precipitation, including snow, is approximately 50 cm (20 in) in this region. However, excessive precipitation from two recent storms caused debris flows in Coronado National Memorial. Debris flows from these two storms rampaged down Montezuma Canyon and damaged roads, campgrounds, and other infrastructure in the memorial.

In the first of these recent storms, the park received 39.29 cm (15.47 in) of precipitation from July 26 to August 5, 2006. This storm caused 113 slope failures in the Huachuca Mountains, within and adjacent to Coronado National Memorial (fig. 7). Only one-third of the debris flows in the memorial originated in burned areas (Webb et al. 2008).

On July 31, 2006, 14 large debris flows inundated part of Montezuma Canyon Road. Flooding caused the road to buckle, snap, and erode at more than 20 points along a 5-km (3-mi) stretch (fig. 8). The debris flow cut through the edge of the picnic area, washing away picnic tables and grills and leaving an arroyo up to 4.5 m (15 ft) deep (fig. 8). In the flood, a well pump house originally located near a normally dry wash was displaced and partially buried in sediment. Coronado National Memorial re-opened to the public after 4 months of repair work (Pearthree and Youberg 2006). Significant debris flows associated with the July 2006 storm also swept through other National Park Service units in Arizona including Saguaro National Park (Graham 2010), Fort Bowie National Historic Site (Graham 2011b), and near Tumacácori National Historical Park (Graham 2011a).

Heavy rainfall [9.32 cm (3.67 in)] on July 27, 2008 again caused debris flows in Coronado National Memorial (fig. 9). The flood tore asphalt from Montezuma Canyon Road, eroded the roadbed, and spread boulders and other debris on the pavement. In September 2009, volunteers rehabilitated a portion of the Cave Trail that had suffered damage from the 2008 flood.

Prior to these storms, numerous debris flows occurred in the southern Huachuca Mountains during the summer rainy seasons of 1977 and 1988 and following major forest-fire events (Wohl and Pearthree 1991). The massive Monument fire of June and July 2011—which closed the memorial—greatly impacted vegetation and created increased concern for subsequent debris flows.

Debris flows in other regions of Arizona provide instructive examples of the potential scale of these geologic hazards. During the final week of 2006, an unusual weather pattern produced several days of nocturnal and early-morning rainfall in southeastern Arizona. Some mountainous areas received up to 20 cm (8 in) of rainfall in less than 6 hours; such extreme quantities are 400- to 1,200-year events (Pearthree and Youberg 2006; Webb et al. 2008). The most intense associated debris-flow activity occurred in the Santa Catalina Mountains near Tucson, where debris flows resulting from 435 slope failures released an estimated 1.5 million tons of sediment into the channels of 10 drainage basins (Webb et al. 2008; Youberg et al. 2008). Despite the potential local impact of recent wildfires, this historically unprecedented quantity of slope failures and debris flows was caused primarily by extreme precipitation (Webb et al. 2008; Youberg et al. 2008).

Debris flows generate tremendous quantities of sediment and move large amounts of material in exceptionally short periods of time. In mountainous areas, they may be the most important mechanism for sediment transfer from hillslopes to larger streams (Wohl and Pearthree 1991; Pearthree and Youberg 2006). Discharge of the July 31, 2006 flood measured 402 m³/s (14,200 ft³/s) at the San Pedro River gauging station in Palominas, Arizona, located about 16 km (10 mi) east of the memorial (Webb et al. 2008). Disregarding atypical runoff events, annual discharge at Palominas from 2005 through 2009 ranged from 0.018 m³/s (0.64 ft³/s) in 2009 to 0.065 m³/s (2.3 ft³/s) in 2008 (U.S. Geological Survey 2010). Runoff data have not been collected from watersheds within the memorial.

In August 2009, the park announced a project designed to: 1) repair streams, 2) grade channels and protect embankments within Montezuma Creek, 3) construct new low water-crossings, and 4) repair the pavement of the Montezuma Canyon and picnic access roads. The following repairs had been completed by April 2010 (Hall 2010):

- Repaving of the park road,

- Installment of low-water crossings,

- Installment of turnouts along the roadway,

- Rehabilitation of the picnic area,

- Construction of a new Coronado Cave trailhead and trail outside of the main drainage area to reduce future repair costs.

The park also received Federal Highway Administration funds to clear and realign the main river channel in the park.

Older debris flows are mapped in the included digital geologic map data (GIS) as map unit Qd.

Rockfalls

Although rockfalls are not a major issue in Coronado National Memorial, steep basalt cliffs in Carr Canyon, and possibly in other canyons, display landslide potential (Floyd Gray, Geologist, U.S. Geological Survey, personal

communication, April 6, 2006). Rockfalls and associated landslides in these canyons might damage roads and trails. Reactivation of older Quaternary landslide deposits in the Glance Conglomerate (map unit Jg) may also present a minor geologic hazard.

Monitoring

Wieczorek and Snyder (2009) described the various types of slope movements and mass-wasting triggers, and suggested the use of five vital signs to monitor slope movements: 1) type of landslide, 2) landslide triggers and causes, 3) geologic material components, 4) landslide movement, and 5) landslide hazards and risks. Their publication provides guidance for the measurement of vital signs and describes a monitoring methodology.

Abandoned Mineral Lands

The Huachuca Mountains management unit of the Coronado Forest contains the New Reef (tungsten) and New Hartford (other minerals) mineral districts. Lead, zinc, copper, silver, and gold were produced in the Hartford mineral district from the late 1800s to the 1960s. Although minor amounts of precious and base-metals were produced in the New Reef mineral district in the early 1900s, tungsten production became the primary activity in this district during World War I. A 1994 appraisal of these districts (Tuftin and Armstrong 1994) found no areas containing economic mineral resources that warranted mineral exploration or mining activity.

By the mid-1970s, the Department of the Interior had evaluated many mining claims in Coronado National Memorial and found no significant mineral value. The Mining in Parks Act of September 28, 1976 prohibited active mining in National Park Service units. By 1985, the memorial had acquired 21 patented mining claims totaling 392 ha (969 ac) that were located in rangeland downslope from the visitors center added to the memorial following a boundary expansion in 1978 (National Park Service 2006a, 2006b). Geologic processes that generated mineable ore bodies are described in the Features and Processes section.

Coronado National Memorial's inventory of abandoned mineral lands includes 62 mine shafts, adits, and test pits (National Park Service 2007b). The State of Texas Mine within the memorial and the Morgan Mine, located just north of the park in South Fork Canyon, are two of the largest abandoned mines in the area. As early as 1903, the State of Texas Mine included three tunnels, two shafts [one approximately 76 m (250 ft) deep], about 76 m (250 ft) of drifts (underground horizontal openings extending from the shaft to the ore body), and an irregular stope (underground excavation formed by the extraction of ore) that measured approximately 4 m (80 ft) in length and width and 1.5 to 4.6 m (5 to 15 ft) in height (Mindat.org n.d.).

Because they pose a safety hazard to visitors, most mines in the memorial are marked with warning signs and are off-limits to the public. In 1993, the Geologic Resources Division of the National Park Service submitted an

Abandoned Mineral Lands inventory and mitigation report for 36 openings. Many of these were sealed by a volunteer group of retired citizens (Floyd Gray, Geologist, U.S. Geological Survey, personal communication, April 6, 2006). Some particularly dangerous shafts and adits were closed with cable nets and bat-friendly gates (National Park Service 2006b), but many of these cable nets were subsequently vandalized and bypassed (John Burghardt, Geologist, NPS Geologic Resources Division, written communication, April 30, 2010).

In 2007, park management submitted an environmental assessment that recommended the closure of four abandoned mine adits along the Crest Trail (a section of the Arizona Trail) (National Park Service 2007b). The recommended approach included the installation of bat-friendly steel gates at the entrances to three of these mines, which deny access to people while providing access to bats and other small animals. The fourth adit, which is small and consists of two branches, was to be filled with rock from the adjacent area and marked with a "Danger, Keep Out" sign. The bat-friendly gates were installed and the fourth adit was partially backfilled in September 2008. In 2010, the gates were armored with reinforced welding that prevents hacksaw vandalism and the backfilled adit was closed with steel grating, using funding obtained through the 2009 American Recovery and Reinvestment Act (ARRA) (John Burghardt, Geologist, NPS Geologic Resources Division, written communication, April 30, 2010).

ARRA funds were also used to close the State of Texas Mine. Closure of the State of Texas Mine was especially significant because the mine hosts a seasonal colony of up to 30,000 lesser long-nosed bats (*Leptonycteris curasoae yerbabuenae*), which are considered endangered under the federal Endangered Species Act. This colony of nectar-feeding bats migrates north from Mexico each summer in pursuit of agave and other cactus blooms. As the undocumented immigrant issue escalates in this region, the prohibition of human access to the State of Texas Mine was imperative for the protection of the bat colony.

In addition to the State of Texas Mine, the ARRA funds allowed the park to close and mitigate all the abandoned mineral lands in Coronado National Memorial (Linda Dansby, Regional Minerals Coordinator, NPS Intermountain Region, personal communication, May 12, 2011). The abandoned mineral lands were closed by partial or complete backfilling, polyurethane plugs, bat gates, and cupolas that were especially designed for each case. Specific design parameters may be obtained by contacting Linda Dansby, Regional Minerals Coordinator, at the NPS Intermountain Region in Santa Fe, New Mexico.

Preservation of Paleontological Resources (Fossils)

The Paleozoic limestones in the Huachuca Mountains, and throughout Arizona, preserve fossils of a variety of marine invertebrates. The fossils in the park have not

been surveyed or adequately interpreted. Features resembling algal stromatolites (layered deposits of blue-green algae) are exposed in limestone and dolomite blocks near the entrance of Coronado Cave. These fossils are usually difficult to remove from the rock matrix, minimizing unauthorized collecting.

In Coronado National Memorial, contact metamorphism from igneous intrusions, volcanic activity, deformation from faulting, and recrystalization of limestone to dolomite destroyed many fossils (Charles Ferguson, Arizona Geological Survey, and Floyd Gray, Geologist, U.S. Geological Survey, personal communication, April 2006). Currently, fossil collecting is not a major issue for Coronado National Memorial resource management.

The 2009 Paleontological Resources Preservation Act directs the National Park Service to manage and protect paleontological resources using science-based principles and expertise. It also calls for inventory, monitoring, and scientific and educational use of fossil resources. Protection of associated location information is also required, as fossils are non-renewable resources. The National Park Service and other federal land management agencies are currently (August 2011) developing joint regulations associated with the Act.

Tweet et al. (2008) summarized the known and potential paleontological resources of the NPS Sonoran Desert Inventory and Monitoring Network, including Coronado National Memorial. Santucci et al. (2009) have outlined the potential threats to in-situ paleontological resources and suggested the use of vital signs to qualitatively and quantitatively monitor the potential impacts of these threats. Paleontological vital signs include: 1) erosion (geologic factors), 2) erosion (climatic factors), 3) catastrophic geohazards, 4) hydrology/bathymetry, and 5) human access/public use. The authors have also presented detailed methodologies for vital-sign monitoring.

Seismic Activity (Earthquakes)

Seismic activity is extremely rare in the Coronado National Memorial region and throughout southeastern Arizona (Arizona Earthquake Information Center 2010). Fourteen earthquakes in the 20th century produced minor tremors in Arizona, most affecting northern or north-central Arizona (U.S. Geological Survey 2009).

The most famous earthquake to shake southeastern Arizona was the 1887 Sonora earthquake. Ground-shaking damaged buildings throughout the sparsely populated region. The fault scarp along the eastern side of the San Bernardino Valley in northeastern Sonora, Mexico, was 50 km (31 mi) long and reached a maximum height of 4 m (13 ft) (Sumner 1977). The San Bernardino Valley forms part of a long, continuous rift valley that extends into the Basin and Range Province of Arizona. Although this province remains tectonically active, such tectonic activity is infrequent in Arizona. For more information regarding seismic activity in Arizona, visit the U.S. Geological Survey Earthquake Hazards Program website: http://earthquake.usgs.gov/earthquakes/states/ (accessed August 15, 2011).

Undocumented Immigrants and Safety Issues

Drug smuggling, human trafficking, and the passage of undocumented immigrants from Mexico into the United States present visitor safety issues at Coronado National Memorial, may disturb research projects in some canyons, and disrupt bat habitat. To evade law enforcement personnel, drug and human smugglers have been forced to select more rugged routes, such as the Crest Trail. In the past, undocumented immigrants and smugglers have used the mines in Coronado National Memorial and surrounding lands for shelter and to store contraband (John Burghardt, Geologist, NPS Geologic Resources Division, written communication, April 30, 2010).

Closure of the abandoned mine openings should decrease and potentially eliminate the use of these mines by undocumented immigrants and smugglers. The bat-friendly gates should protect bat and small-animal habitat while enhancing the safety of visitors and law-enforcement staff (John Burghardt, Geologist, NPS Geologic Resources Division, written communication, April 30, 2010).

Table 1. Heavy metal contamination in surface water samples, Coronado National Memorial.

Site	Sampling Year	Heavy Metal	Sample Value	EPA MCL	
				Drinking Water	Acute Freshwater
CORO0004	1993	Beryllium	22	4	
		Cadmium	164	5	3.9
		Copper	120,950	1,300	18
		Lead	44	15	
		Selenium	106	50	20
		Silver	43		4.1
		Zinc	32,690	5,000	120
CORO0005	1993	Copper	497	1,300	18
		Zinc	426	5,000	120
CORO0006	1993	Copper	381	1,300	18
Blue Waterfall seep (2 sites)	2003	Cadmium	29	5	3.9
		Copper	505	1,300	18
		Zinc	3,650	5,000	120
State of Texas mine	2003	Uranium	12.2		
			113		
			122		
			122		
Fern Grotto (Brown allotment)	2003	Uranium	11.4		
			11.7		
			10.2	10	
Yaqui Spring	2003	Uranium	23.4		
Joe's Spring	2003	Uranium	58.6		
			13.2		
Clark-Smith mine	2003	Uranium	36.7		
			37.8		
			30.0		

1993 data are from the NPS Water Resources Division (2000) and 2003 data are from the U.S. Geological Survey (Brown 2005). Values recorded in micrograms per liter. MCL = Maximum Contaminant Level.

Figure 7. Debris flow chutes on the east face of Montezuma Peak caused by slope failure in 2006. Rushing debris flows eroded all the vegetation, leaving new Y-shaped chutes beneath granite outcrops. The debris flows originated in an area that had not recently burned. National Park Service photograph, available online: http://www.nps.gov/coro/photosmultimedia/2006-Flood-Damage.htm (accessed August 15, 2011).

Figure 8. Destruction produced by the July 31, 2006 debris flow and flooding. (A) Water flowed across the Montezuma Canyon Road. The debris flow deposited rocks on the road and caused the road to buckle, snap, and erode in more than 20 points along a 5-km (3-mi) stretch. (B) The picnic area was severely damaged by a debris flow that swept away several picnic tables, broke water lines, destroyed trail access to the picnic area, and carved a path along the edge of this picnic area. Note the picnic table at the edge of the steep, eroded bank. The flood cut an arroyo that was up to 4.6 m (15 ft) deep. National Park Service photographs, available online: http://www.nps.gov/coro/photosmultimedia/2006-Flood-Damage.htm (accessed August 15, 2011).

07/28/2008

Figure 9. Damage from the July, 2008 debris flow. Flood waters ripped up asphalt, scattered rocks on the pavement, eroded the roadbed, and carved a 1.5-m (5-ft) trench through the roadway. National Park Service photograph, available online: http://www.nps.gov/coro/photosmultimedia/2008-Flood-Damage-Gallery.htm (accessed August 15, 2011).

Geologic Features and Processes

This section describes the most prominent and distinctive geologic features and processes in Coronado National Memorial.

Coronado National Memorial contains geologic features that reflect a wide variety of geologic processes, from cataclysmic volcanic eruptions to gradual formation of limestone at the bottom of ancient seas. Dissolution of calcium carbonate carved modern caves in limestone blocks that are approximately 300 million years old. Tectonic activity resulted in the Huachuca Mountains. Ephemeral stream channels have been altered recently by rare debris flows. The memorial preserves these features and protects an outdoor laboratory where researchers may study processes that have occurred throughout geologic time.

Coronado Cave

Coronado Cave begins at the end of a 1.2-km (0.75-mi)-long trail that starts at the Visitor Center. A jumble of limestone blocks marks the entrance to the cave (map unit PZl). Several crawl ways and short passages branch from the main body of the cave, which measures approximately 180 m (600 ft) long, 6 m (20 ft) high, and 21 m (70 ft) wide.

Coronado Cave provides visitors with the opportunity to view a variety of cave formations (speleothems), including stalactites, stalagmites, flowstones, and helictites. Massive calcite columns have formed when a stalactite and stalagmite meet (fig. 10). Rimstone dams have created ridges of calcite that retain pools of water in the rear portion of Coronado Cave.

Coronado Cave developed in Paleozoic limestone of the Naco Group (map unit PZl). About 250 to 300 million years ago, a shallow sea covering southern Arizona hosted Paleozoic corals, sponges, shellfish, and other marine invertebrates. The shells and exoskeletons of these animals formed from calcium and carbon dioxide dissolved in seawater. The remains of these invertebrates settled to the sea floor, were broken by waves into sand- and silt-sized particles, and finally hardened into limestone when compacted by younger sediments.

By the Early Triassic (251 to 246 million years ago), the shallow sea had retreated from southern Arizona. In the Jurassic (200 to 145 million years ago), violent volcanic eruptions in the region produced extensive calderas and granitic intrusions (see below). Magma that formed the Huachuca granite (map unit Jh) intruded into the Naco Group limestone, forming the currently visible lenses of whitish to grayish limestones encased by tan to brown granite (Hon et al. 2007).

Coronado Cave was formed by water seeping down from the mountains through cracks in the limestone. Caves typically form near the level where rocks are saturated with water. Rainwater becomes slightly acidic as it absorbs carbon dioxide from the atmosphere and percolates through soils that are rich in carbon dioxide released by insects, bacteria, and plant roots. This slightly acidic groundwater dissolves individual calcite grains in the limestone.

Cave formation at Coronado National Memorial has been enhanced by the reaction of iron sulfides (primarily pyrite) with percolating groundwater. When the limestone reacted with the enclosing Huachuca granite, magnetite, hematite, and iron-sulfide replacement skarn bodies formed locally along the margins of the limestone blocks (Hon et al. 2007). Through a series of chemical reactions, pyrite reacted with groundwater to form sulfuric acid. The welling up of this acid from beneath the cave dissolved the limestone to help create the passages and caverns currently exposed in Coronado Cave (National Park Service n.d.).

In addition to the small-scale processes that formed the cave, larger-scale processes helped shape the cave. Limestone bedding planes in Coronado Cave exhibit scalloped surfaces formed by an estimated 190,000 L/min (50,000 gal/min) of water that flowed from east to west through the cave (National Park Service n.d.).

The dust that covers the speleothems in Coronado Cave detracts from their appearance and impedes their rate of growth. Water supply, cave humidity, surface soils, bacteria, and limestone composition influence the rate at which speleothems grow. A cave restoration program could enhance protection of these geologic features.

Montezuma Caldera

Calderas are evidence of one of nature's most violent volcanic processes. Calderas form following a tremendous volcanic eruption that removes large volumes of magma from the underlying magma chamber, causing the volcano to collapse as rubble into the chamber. Extraordinary amounts of debris and ash-flows are produced and harden into "tuff." The rubble that collapses back into the crater is termed "collapse breccia." Particularly large blocks of rubble are "megabreccia."

Calderas differ from volcanic craters, which form at the summit of a volcanic cone following an eruption. Most craters are the remnants of the conduit, or volcanic vent, through which magma flowed. The diameter of a caldera is many times greater than that of a volcanic vent. A caldera eruption created the basin that now hosts Crater Lake in Crater Lake National Park (Oregon; fig. 11). The Yellowstone hotspot beneath Yellowstone National Park (Wyoming, Montana, Idaho) produced a number of immense caldera eruptions.

In the Early and Middle Jurassic (200 to 161 million years ago), subduction along the active plate-tectonic margin of western North America initiated cataclysmic volcanic eruptions that produced three overlapping calderas (Montezuma, Turkey Canyon, Parker Canyon) in the southern Huachuca Mountains and neighboring Canelo Hills, approximately 21 km (13 mi) northwest of the memorial (Lipman and Hagstrum 1992; Hon and Lipman 1994). Coronado National Memorial lies entirely within the Montezuma Caldera, the oldest of the three features. Evidence of the collapse that formed the Montezuma Caldera can be found in the caldera-collapse breccia ("Jmb" map units; further described below) exposed south of Montezuma Canyon and accessible using Joe's Canyon Trail (Hon et al. 2007). The megabreccia found in Coronado National Memorial consists of exceptionally large angular clasts.

Erosion and subsequent tectonic events have obscured the southwestern half of the Montezuma Caldera, but exposures in the southern Huachuca Mountains suggest that it was approximately 16 to 18 km (10 to 11 mi) in diameter (Lipman and Hagstrum 1992). The 26.9-million-year-old Turkey Creek Caldera, which forms much of the landscape in Chiricahua National Monument, has a comparable diameter of approximately 19 km (12 mi) wide (Drewes 1982; Kring 2002; Graham 2009).

Montezuma Caldera Crystal-rich Dacite Tuff

The three caldera-forming volcanic episodes in the southern Huachuca Mountains produced densely welded ash-flow tuffs. Welded tuff is the product of volcanic ash and particles that fuse together while extremely hot. Ash-flows consist of a hot mixture of volcanic gases and pyroclastic material traveling across the ground surface. The ash-flows associated with the Montezuma Caldera may be described as ignimbrite outflow sheets, due to the large volumes of volcanic material (10s to 100s of km^3) that they contained (Michael Conway, Geologist, Arizona Geological Survey, written communication, February 27, 2011). In general, the explosive disintegration of viscous, gas-rich magma in a volcanic crater or fissure often results in ash-flows. These flows may include an unsorted assemblage of volcanic dust, pumice, scoria, volcanic blocks, and individual minerals such as quartz, biotite, albite, and sanidine.

The oldest Jurassic ash-flow sheet in the area (map unit Jhl) is characterized by a crystal-rich dacite tuff containing abundant phenocrysts (crystals larger than the enclosing matrix) of plagioclase, biotite, and quartz. In Montezuma Canyon, the densely welded, red-brown, dacitic ash-flow tuff is more than 1,400 m (4,600 ft) thick (Lipman and Hagstrum 1992).

South of Montezuma Canyon, the uppermost section of the crystal-rich dacite tuff displays parallel color-banded layers of reddish-brown to reddish-gray tuff. Interbedded caldera-collapse breccias (map unit Jmbls)

composed of shattered limestone and pre-caldera andesite and dacite lavas form distinct layers within the banded dacite tuff. Crystal-poor rhyolite tuff of the younger Turkey Canyon Caldera (map unit Jrt) overlies the crystal-rich dacite tuff in this area (Hon et al. 2007).

Metamorphism appears to have influenced the dacite tuff in the northern part of Coronado National Memorial more than indicated by exposures to the south. The ridge to Montezuma Peak contains dark-greenish-gray dacite tuff that has undergone low-pressure-temperature alteration. The mineral epidote coats the abundant fractures, and the tuff has been metamorphosed to hornfels near contacts with the Huachuca granite (Hon et al. 2007). The tuff also contains abundant rock debris and huge, megabreccia blocks of pre-caldera andesite and limestone ranging from 30 to 500 m (100 to 1,600 ft) thick. The degree of metamorphic alteration and the coarse, equigranular texture of the Huachuca granite (map unit Jhgb) suggest that the dacite tuff near Montezuma Peak originally extruded into the deepest part of the caldera (Hon et al. 2007).

Caldera-collapse breccia (map units Jmbls, Jmbcs, Jmbsr) interfingers with the crystal-rich dacite tuff on Bob Thompson Peak, north of a major thrust fault (fig. 5) that has been mapped in the area (Drewes 1980; Hon et al. 2007). East of Miller Peak, the tuff overlies a thick stratigraphic section containing large blocks of limestone breccia. Low-grade metamorphism associated with the regional thrust fault generated minerals, such as epidote and chlorite that give the tuff its green color. Pods of poorly welded tuff exhibit a phyllitic texture in which individual crystals share a slightly parallel orientation.

Volcanic eruptions also occurred about this time in the Mustang Mountains, approximately 40 km (25 mi) north of the memorial. The red-brown to green dacite tuff of the Montezuma Caldera (map unit Jhl) correlates with the thin outflow sheet of dacite tuff found in the Mustang Mountains (Lipman and Hagstrum 1992; Hon et al. 2007).

Montezuma Caldera Collapse Breccia

Crystal-rich dacite tuff and collapse breccia record synchronous infilling of the collapsing Montezuma Caldera. Caldera collapse produced shattered masses and chaotic landslide blocks of pre-existing rocks consisting of Paleozoic limestone, dolomite, and sandstone, and Jurassic and possibly Triassic sandstone, siltstone, and limestone conglomerate (Lipman and Hagstrum 1992; Hon and Lipman 1994; Hon et al. 2007). As an illustration of the power of the caldera eruption, the Paleozoic carbonate megabreccia, some of which is comprised of composite aggregates of multiple blocks of rock, reaches lengths of 2 km (1.2 mi) (Lipman and Hagstrum 1992; Hon and Lipman 1994).

Within Coronado National Memorial, dark-gray to white masses of Paleozoic limestone (map unit Jmbls) form aggregates of broken and shattered blocks as long as 1 km (0.6 mi) (Hon et al. 2007). Limestone and andesite are mixed in thick breccia lenses south of Montezuma Canyon. Near Miller Peak, dacite tuff completely encloses smaller limestone masses. North of the memorial, near Bob Thompson Peak, the limestone has been metamorphosed and recrystallized to marble. As noted above, Coronado Cave did not form in one of these shattered limestone blocks, but lies within an intact lens of limestone surrounded by Huachuca granite.

Previous mapping identified thick sections of undisturbed limestones exposed east of Miller Peak, west of Copper Canyon, and south of Montezuma Canyon as undifferentiated members of the Paleozoic Naco Group. However, several lines of evidence, including the irregular pods and lenses of calcite tuff, volcanic rock inclusions, random bedding orientations of some blocks, shattered textures, and diverse rock types (e.g., sandstone surrounded by larger blocks of limestone) suggest that these deposits are thick accumulations of megabreccia (Hon et al. 2007).

Shattered blocks of reddish-brown to dark-gray andesite and dacite lava form lenses of collapse breccia south of Montezuma Canyon and between Montezuma Pass and Miller Peak (map unit Jmbmv). Andesite and dacite are fine-grained, extrusive igneous rocks that contain less quartz than does rhyolite, the volcanic equivalent of granite; the darker andesite contains more calcic plagioclase (a feldspar mineral) and less quartz than does dacite. Andesite and dacite contain less quartz than rhyolite, the volcanic equivalent to granite. Small, isolated exposures of reddish-brown to dark-gray lava are also present near Bob Thompson Peak (Hon et al. 2007). Some contain plagioclase phenocrysts and others are aphanitic, lacking phenocrysts. The abundance of these disturbed volcanic blocks near the southern margin of the Montezuma Caldera suggests that several volcanic centers may have been present in this area prior to caldera collapse.

Laminated sandstone, siltstone, shale, marl, and limestone-clast conglomerate form large blocks of collapse breccia north of the major thrust fault mapped in the northeastern sector of the memorial (map unit Jmbsr). Like other collapse breccia, this unit does not exist outside of the caldera. Although the variety of rock types resembles that of the Cretaceous Morita Formation (map unit Km), the megablocks within the Montezuma Caldera must have been deposited during the Jurassic or Triassic (Hon et al. 2007). Evidence of old soil development in the matrix of the limestone conglomerate suggests that this conglomerate may have formed on an ancient karst landscape surface dating to a previous erosional episode before the caldera collapse.

Fine-grained hornfels with boulder to megablock inclusions of recrystallized limestone (map unit Jmbcs) encircle Bob Thompson Peak but are exposed primarily north of the memorial. The original argillaceous (clayey) limestone was probably metamorphosed by hot fluids during cooling of the intra-caldera fill sequence. Adjacent to the Huachuca granite, contact metamorphism produced a calc-silicate rock containing the minerals garnet, vesuvianite, epidote, and pyroxene.

The hornfels on Bob Thompson Peak have been crushed and sheared and are strongly foliated. In contrast, the large limestone inclusions have been deformed plastically. The contrast between the dense hornfels and less-competent limestone inclusions has given the unit the appearance of a crude flow structure. Pods of dacite tuff within this sequence have been metamorphosed to phyllite and form a well-developed boudinage structure, wherein less competent units have been stretched, thinned, and broken at regular intervals into blocks that resemble boudins or sausages (Hon et al. 2007).

Volcanic Deposits of the Turkey Canyon Caldera

Within Coronado National Memorial, a 35-m- (115-ft-) thick layer of crystal-poor rhyolite tuff (map unit Jrt) from the Turkey Canyon eruption directly overlies Montezuma Caldera crystal-rich dacite tuff south of Montezuma Canyon (Lipman and Hagstrum 1992; Hon et al. 2007). The welded tuff is color-banded but does not show signs of internal ductile flow that is characteristic of the tuff in Turkey Canyon. Prior to deposition of the Turkey Canyon Caldera tuff, the upper 1 to 2 m (3.3 to 6.6 ft) of crystal-rich dacite tuff had been locally reworked by stream flow.

In the Turkey Canyon area of the southern Canelo Hills, a distinctive gray to red-gray, crystal-poor rhyolite tuff marks the eruptive episode that produced the Turkey Canyon Caldera. The welded tuff contains textures that suggest it underwent ductile flow before it solidified. Hollow, bubble-like structures indicate high volatile contents (gas) in the original tuff. Outflow volcanic tuffs with ductile flow characteristics are also exposed in the Mustang Mountains to the north of the memorial (Hon and Lipman 1994).

In the western United States, similar ductile, crystal-poor rhyolite tuffs erupted during the Paleogene (65 to 23 million years ago) at temperatures ranging from 800°C to 900°C (1,500°F to 1,700°F). The lithologic and textural similarity between these Paleogene and Mesozoic tuffs suggests that these relatively high temperatures may also have characterized the eruption of rhyolite tuffs in Turkey Canyon (Hon and Lipman 1994).

Volcanic Deposits of the Parker Canyon Caldera

The uppermost (youngest) major ash-flow sheet in the southern Huachuca Mountains consists of a red-brown, quartz-rich, quartz-rhyolite welded tuff that erupted from the area of Parker Canyon in the Canelo Hills (map unit Jpt). This tuff ponded within the Montezuma Caldera in the Coronado National Memorial area and overlies tuffs of the older Turkey Canyon and Montezuma calderas in the Huachuca and Mustang Mountains (Lipman and Hagstrum 1992; Hon et al. 2007).

Previously mapped as the welded tuff member of the Canelo Hills Volcanics (Hayes 1970), the tuff contains phenocrysts of primarily quartz and potassium feldspar and minor crystals of plagioclase and biotite (Hon et al. 2007). In Coronado National Memorial, the Parker Canyon ash-flow tuff forms a 30- to 40-m- (100- to 130-ft) thick continuous exposure above the Turkey Canyon tuff on the south side of Montezuma Canyon (map unit Jpt) (Hon et al. 2007).

Thin beds of pink to pinkish-gray, poorly- to moderately-welded ash-flow tuffs containing abundant rock fragments and small [1- to 2-mm (0.04- to 0.08-in)] phenocrysts of quartz and potassium feldspar underlie the Parker Canyon Caldera volcanic rocks (map unit Jqlt). These lithic-rich tuffs are similar to the rhyolite tuffs found at the base of the Parker Canyon sequence, suggesting that they represent early volcanic eruptions that led to the formation of the Parker Canyon Caldera. Thin layers of ash-fall tuffs are mixed in with the ash-flow tuffs (Hon et al. 2007). Some exposures display a gradual transition from the lithic-rich tuffs to the overlying Parker Canyon rhyolite tuff, but 5 to 10 m (16 to 33 ft) of sediment separate the two units in other locations (Hon et al. 2007).

Approximately 10 to 33 m (33 to 100 ft) of orange to red-orange, feldspar- and quartz-rich sandstones, siltstones, and conglomerates separate the lithic-rich ash-flow tuffs and Parker Canyon Caldera rhyolite ash-flow tuffs from the underlying Turkey Canyon rhyolite (fig. 4). Some of the very well-sorted quartz sandstone may represent eolian deposits (Hon et al. 2007).

Joe's Canyon Trail traverses exposures of the Parker Canyon and Turkey Canyon tuffs, as well as the sandstone and lithic-rich tuffs that separate the units.

Huachuca Granite

Following the collapse of the Montezuma Caldera, Huachuca granite intruded into the dacite tuff. Two types of Huachuca granite are exposed in Coronado National Memorial: porphyritic granite (map unit Jhgp) and equigranular granite (map unit Jhgb) (Hon and Lipman 1994; Hon et al. 2007). Porphyritic granite is characterized by large mineral crystals surrounded by a much finer (smaller) grained texture. Mineral crystals in equigranular granite are all of similar sizes. Both types consist of medium- to- coarse-grained granite exposed north of Montezuma Canyon, and have been intruded by east–west trending mafic dikes. The sequence of these granites remains undetermined.

Porphyritic granite is exposed east of Montezuma Peak but cannot be easily accessed by a developed trail. Phenocrysts in the porphyritic granite are composed primarily of 2- to 3-cm (0.8- to 1.2-in) orthoclase feldspar crystals. In contrast to granite porphyry, the porphyritic granite has fewer phenocrysts and a coarser-grained matrix [5 mm (0.2 in)] of feldspar, quartz, biotite, and amphibole minerals.

Equigranular granite can be seen along the Coronado Cave Trail. Coronado Cave is surrounded by pink to pinkish-gray equigranular granite, which is the dominant phase exposed within the memorial. The granite consists of roughly equal amounts of potassium and plagioclase feldspars and quartz, and minor amounts of biotite (Hon et al. 2007).

Mineralization

Mineralization refers to any of a variety of processes where minerals, particularly economically valuable ones, are introduced into surrounding rock. Copper mineralization occurred at the contact of limestone strata with Jurassic-age plutons near Bisbee, Arizona, approximately 39 km (24 mi) east of the memorial across the San Pedro Valley. Volcanic eruptions and subsequent development of the Montezuma Caldera, however, prevented significant copper mineralization in the southern Huachuca Mountains (Hon and Lipman 1994). The Turkey Canyon and Parker Canyon calderas show no evidence of associated metallic mineralization (Lipman and Hagstrum 1992).

Hydrothermal solutions resulting from a late-Jurassic intrusion and dike swarm are responsible for the ore deposits in the southern Huachuca Mountains. Hydrothermal activity scavenged enough zinc, silver, gold, copper, and other metallic elements from the dacite tuff to produce small skarn (calcium-bearing silicate) deposits. Skarn deposits derive from the introduction of large amounts of silica, aluminum, iron, and magnesium into nearly pure limestone or dolomite. Most mining in the region exploited skarn deposits that formed at the contact of igneous intrusions with sedimentary strata, especially limestone (Charles Ferguson, Arizona Geological Survey, personal communication, April 2006).

For example, deposits in the State of Texas Mine show that metallic-rich hydrothermal solutions circulating through cracks and fissures at the contact between the Huachuca granite (map unit Jhgb) and the Naco Group limestone (map unit PZl) replaced the limestone with ore deposits. The best-developed mineralization can be observed in two nearly vertical, northwest-trending fissure zones situated about 7.6 m (25 ft) apart (Mindat.org n.d.).

Spaniards may have been the first prospectors to work what is now the State of Texas Mine in the 17th century. However, the first recorded ore production occurred in the 1880s. Sporadic production occurred until 1943 when mining activity increased significantly to provide zinc and lead for World War II (National Park Service 2006b). Closed to mining by the 1976 Mining in Parks Act, these abandoned mines currently present water-quality and visitor-safety issues (see the Geologic Issues section for further information).

Sedimentary Rock Features

The youngest sedimentary rock in Coronado National Memorial is the Cretaceous Morita Formation (map unit Km) of the Bisbee Group (fig. 4). The Morita Formation overlies the latest Jurassic to Early Cretaceous Glance Conglomerate (map units Jg, Jga), which forms the base of the Bisbee Group. Two other Cretaceous-aged formations in the Bisbee Group, the Mural Limestone (map unit Kmu) and the Cintura Formation (map unit Kc), are exposed within the Huachuca Mountains but not within the memorial. The oldest sedimentary units in the memorial are the Paleozoic limestones and dolomitic limestones that are surrounded by the Huachuca granite. In Coronado National Memorial, these isolated limestone blocks belong to the Pennsylvanian- to- Permian-aged Naco Group (map unit PZl) (fig. 4). The caves in Coronado National Memorial, including Coronado Cave, developed in these limestone deposits.

Morita Formation (Cretaceous)

Morita Formation sandstone, siltstone, and shale occur in a complexly faulted outcrop belt within a narrow, northwest-trending fault zone that parallels Montezuma Canyon. Outside of the memorial, the Morita Formation is 1,280 m (4,200 ft) thick on the western slopes of the Huachuca Mountains (Hayes 1970). The formation consists of well-sorted quartz sandstones interbedded with red to maroon siltstone and shale (Hon et al. 2007). Horizontal fractures cut through the shale layers, but rest at high angles to the sandstone beds. Fragments of petrified wood have been found in some of the coarser sandstone beds (although not in the memorial). Thin, silty, oyster-bearing limestone beds occur in the upper part of the formation (Hayes 1970). The base of the formation includes a conglomerate bed containing well-rounded chert fragments (Hon et al. 2007).

Morita Formation rocks visible in Coronado National Memorial record the subsidence of a deltaic plain in southeastern Arizona during the early Cretaceous. Sand filled the channels of streams that flowed across the plain and periodic floods deposited mud and silt. The oyster-bearing limestone beds record intermittent flooding of the delta by brackish water as the sea advanced into the area from the southeast (Hayes 1970).

Glance Conglomerate (latest Jurassic to Early Cretaceous)

The primary sedimentary rock unit in the memorial is the the Glance Conglomerate (map unit Jg; fig. 12). The unit is labeled as the "Glance Formation, volcaniclastic conglomerate member" in the attached GIS data. The conglomerate unit is composed of volcanic clasts, intrusions of basaltic andesite, and a chaotic mixture of landslide blocks that suggest renewed seismic activity in the Montezuma Caldera following its formation earlier in the Jurassic (Hon et al. 2007). The unit is mapped in the southwest portion of the monument and underlies Coronado Peak and Montezuma Pass (see Geologic Map Data section).

Deposition of the Glance Conglomerate occurred within the context of extensional tectonic forces in southeastern Arizona. The boulders and cobbles in the Glance Conglomerate were deposited in alluvial fans along the margins of west–northwest-trending, fault-bounded basins (Bilodeau 1982; Bilodeau et al. 1987; Dickinson et al. 1987; Lipman and Hagstrum 1992). Alluvial fans form when streams emerging from the mouths of steep canyons encounter gentler topographic slopes. Flow energy dissipates and sediment fills the shallow channels, causing stream flow paths to shift laterally. Over time, the back-and-forth migration of a stream across a slope forms a fan-shaped feature.

Regionally, the Glance Conglomerate consists primarily of cobble to boulder conglomerate. The poorly sorted conglomerate contains clasts of Mesozoic, Paleozoic, and Precambrian rock units (Hayes 1970; Bilodeau et al. 1987). Most of the conglomerate consists of clasts in contact with one another (clast-supported); sand grains fill the interstices and mineral cement bonds the large clasts and sand grains. Other parts of the conglomerate contain clasts that appear to float within a matrix of sand grains. In southeastern Arizona, the Glance Conglomerate varies in thickness from zero (locally absent) to over 2,000 m (6,600 ft) (Bilodeau et al. 1987).

In the southwestern part of Coronado National Memorial, the Glance Conglomerate unconformably overlies a number of geologic rock units: the Jurassic Parker Canyon Caldera rhyolite tuff (map unit Jpt), the sedimentary unit separating the Parker Canyon and Turkey Canyon tuffs (map unit Jqlt), the Turkey Canyon Caldera rhyolite tuff (map unit Jrt), and the Montezuma Canyon Caldera dacite tuff (map unit Jhl) (Hon et al. 2007).

Non-stratified, matrix-supported conglomerate at the base of the formation gradually yields to crudely stratified, clast-supported conglomerate higher in the unit. The composition of the clasts also varies. Younger Parker Canyon Caldera rhyolite tuff clasts dominate the lower part of the conglomerate, but as erosion exposed older rock units, abundant clasts of Montezuma Caldera dacite tuff and Paleozoic Naco Group limestone become more prevalent in the upper part (Hon et al. 2007). This type of stratigraphic section where older clasts overlie younger clasts is known as inverted stratigraphy. Excellent examples of inverted stratigraphy and the boulder and cobble conglomerate in the Glance Conglomerate may be viewed on the drive to the Montezuma Pass overlook. The Joe's Canyon, Yaqui Ridge, Coronado Peak, and Arizona trails also traverse the Glance Conglomerate.

Glance Conglomerate Landslide Breccia

East of Montezuma Pass and Coronado Peak, a landslide breccia member forms a narrow, north-south trending exposure within the main body of the Glance Conglomerate (map units Jgbr, Jgbd, Jgba, Jgbls). Wedge- and sheet-like breccia deposits contain chaotic blocks of sandstone, rhyolite and dacite tuff, pre-Montezuma Caldera lava clasts, and Paleozoic limestone (Hon et al. 2007). The breccia member thickens from about 30 m (100 ft) near Montezuma Pass to more than 200 m (660 ft) just south of the U.S.–Mexico border.

Field evidence suggests that the Cretaceous landslides may have originated from two primary source areas: 1) a resurgent dome within the Montezuma Caldera to the north of the memorial, and 2) collapse of the caldera's southern rim. The wedge-shaped nature of the deposit and the presence of large limestone masses suggest that the bulk of the material was probably derived from the southern caldera wall (Hon et al. 2007). Interbedded, alluvial fan conglomerate is absent in the landslide member, suggesting nearly instantaneous deposition. An earthquake during the Cretaceous, for example, may have triggered the instantaneous collapse of the caldera's walls and sent boulder-sized chunks of rocks cascading down the steep slopes (Bilodeau et al. 1987; Hon et al. 2007).

Locally, as in Coronado National Memorial, the chaotic landslide breccias in the Glance Formation reflect continuing instability of the Montezuma Caldera walls well into the Cretaceous. Coronado National Memorial offers an excellent location in which to study the sedimentology and origin of these past landslides and conglomerate deposits and to define their place in the regional tectonic environment of southern Arizona during the Jurassic.

Naco Group (Pensylvanian to Permian)
Paleozoic limestone and dolomitic limestone (map unit PZl) in Coronado National Memorial are completely surrounded by Jurassic-aged Huachuca granite (map unit Jhl). The blocks do not contain sufficient stratigraphic and paleontological information to place them within a specific formation in the Naco Group. Most of the limestone has been recrystallized to marble, and the margins of the blocks have reacted locally with adjacent granite to form skarn bodies or hornfels (Hon et al. 2007). Weak copper skarn mineralization has occurred near contacts of limestone megablocks with the pluton in the Montezuma Caldera (Hon and Lipman 1994).

Exposures in the memorial offer an opportunity to study the interaction between granitic intrusions and limestone. Further research may also contribute to a better understanding of the endangered barking frog's (*Craugastor augusti*) preference for cohesive limestone strata over dislocated limestone blocks (National Park Service 2006a).

Geomorphic Features

The slope failures and flooding events described in the Geologic Issues section dramatically altered the geomorphic landscape in Coronado National Memorial. Although they occur rapidly, debris flows are the major channel-forming events in the Huachuca Mountains (Wohl and Pearthree 1991). The investigation of channel deposits in Coronado National Memorial can provide insights into slope weathering, erosion, and the episodic nature of debris flows. As climate continues to change, monitoring these factors may prove useful to resource managers.

As it enters the memorial from San Pedro Valley, the Montezuma Canyon Road crosses terrace gravels deposited by Pleistocene alluvial fans (map units QgM1,

Qgm2). Similar to processes operating during the deposition of the Glance Conglomerate, intermittent seasonal flooding in the Pleistocene carried eroded sediment through the relatively steep, narrow Montezuma Canyon and dumped a sediment load of gravel, sand, and other coarse material on the gentler slope at the mouth of the canyon. Silt and clay particles were transported farther down the slope. The finer-grained material was deposited as ephemeral stream flow abated, leaving a sediment-choked arroyo. Alluvial fans form distinctive features that rim the basins in the Basin and Range Province (fig. 13). The coalescence of alluvial fans along the border of a basin produces a geomorphic feature known as a bajada.

Laramide Orogeny Features
A change in the angle of the subducting plate along the western margin of North America initiated the Laramide Orogeny approximately 70 million years ago in the Late Cretaceous (see the Geologic History section). The Laramide Orogeny, the most-recent Rocky Mountain-building event, ended about 35 million years ago in the Paleogene. Impressive reverse and thrust faults (fig. 5) related to this orogeny exist in nearly every mountain range in southeastern Arizona, but they have been dissected and moved from their original positions by subsequent basin-and-range faulting.

In Coronado National Memorial, Bob Thompson Peak is located on the hanging wall of the regional, northwest-trending Cochise thrust fault. The movement of this fault transported Jurassic units of collapse-breccia from the Montezuma Caldera over younger Huachuca granite (Drewes 1980; Hon et al. 2007). All of the Hucachuca Mountains (including those on the Cochise thrust fault) form the hanging wall of the low-angled Hidalgo thrust fault, estimated to be 6,800 m (22,300 ft) thick (Drewes 1980). Given the complex geology of the southern Huachuca Mountains, further research is required to establish distinctions between regional tectonic features, such as the Cochise fault, and caldera-related volcanic structures (Lipman and Hagstrum 1994; Hon et al. 2007).

Exposures along the canyon wall near the State of Texas Mine display approximately 18 m (60 ft) of Naco Group marble (metamorphosed limestone) thrust over younger Cretaceous shale and sandstone strata of the Morita Formation. North of the mine, a reverse fault that dips 80° to the north is marked by a copper stain and separates underlying marble from an overlying mass of quartz monzonite (Mindat.org n.d.). Mineralization in the mine is associated with faulting, although it is not clear whether these faults are related to Laramide thrusting and/or younger basin-and-range normal faulting.

Laramide compression also folded the strata into northwest-trending arches (anticlines) and depressions (synclines) in the Huachuca Mountains (fig. 14) (Drewes 1980). Some ore bodies in the State of Texas Mine replaced limestone in the roof of an anticline that tilts gently to the north (Mindat.org n.d.). On a smaller scale,

Laramide deformation flattened and stretched individual limestone cobbles in the Glance Conglomerate (Dickinson et al. 1989).

Basin-and-Range Features

Approximately 20 million years after the end of the Laramide Orogeny, the crust in what is now the southwestern United States began to pull apart. Extension led to today's basin-and-range landscape of adjacent mountain ranges (horsts) and fault-bounded basins (grabens) (fig. 6). Coronado, Miller, and Montezuma peaks in Coronado National Memorial are part of the uplifted horst block of the southern Huachuca Mountains. The mountains are separated from the San Pedro Valley to the east by the north–south-trending Nicksville fault, and a complex zone of normal faults separates the southern Huachuca Mountains and Canelo Hills from the San Rafael de la Zanja to the west (Drewes 1980).

Basin-bounding normal faults may extend thousands of meters into the crust. The Nicksville fault, for example, offsets the Cochise thrust fault at the surface and is projected to intersect and offset the Hidalgo thrust fault at a depth of approximately 4,000 m (13,000 ft) (Drewes 1980). In the southern part of the memorial, however, offset appears to be minor along normal faults that juxtapose Glance Conglomerate with Jurassic sandstone and tuff (Hon et al. 2007).

As part of the isolated Huachuca Mountains, the "sky island" landscape of Coronado National Memorial reflects the tectonic processes that formed the Basin and Range Province (fig. 2). On the northern border of the memorial, Montezuma Peak rises 2,341 m (7,676 ft) above sea level. In contrast, Montezuma Ranch, located at the mouth of Montezuma Canyon, is 1,500 m (5,000 ft) above sea level.

Some areas within the Basin and Range Province continue to experience extension and normal faulting although seismic activity rarely occurs in present-day southeastern Arizona. Today, the trace of the Nicksville fault lies buried beneath alluvial fan deposits (fig. 15).

Figure 10. Limestone column in Coronado Cave. Column formation requires thousands of years of constant dripping. National Park Service photograph by Dave Bly (Coronado National Memorial), available online http://www.nps.gov/coro/naturescience/cave.htm (accessed February 1, 2010).

Figure 11. Crater Lake Caldera, Crater Lake National Park. Like Montezuma Caldera, the Crater Lake Caldera resulted from a tremendous volcanic explosion that removed a large volume of magma from the magma chamber and generated ash, pyroclastic ejecta, pyroclastic flows, and clouds of dense, hot ash that rapidly flowed down the sides of the volcano. Emptied of magma, the magma chamber collapsed and rubble filled the depression. Unlike Montezuma Caldera, Crater Lake caldera was subsequently filled with water, forming the eponymous lake. The diameter of the Crater Lake Caldera is approximately 8 to 10 km (5 to 6 mi). In contrast, the Montezuma Caldera is 16 to 18 km (10 to 11 mi) in diameter. U.S. Geological Survey photograph by Willie Scot, available online: http://vulcan.wr.usgs.gov/Volcanoes/CraterLake/images.html (accessed March 8, 2011).

Figure 12. Glance Conglomerate. This conglomerate is exposed 1.6 km (1 mi) northwest of Gold Hill in the Mule Mountains, approximately 30 km (19 mi) east of Coronado National Memorial, across the San Pedro Valley. At this location, the clasts are composed primarily of metamorphic rock fragments that range from a fraction of a centimeter to 1 m (3 ft) in length (black arrow). Although the composition of the clasts varies, the clasts in the memorial are similar in size and quantity. Photograph by F. L. Ransome, U.S. Geological Survey, November 26, 1902, available online: http://libraryphoto.cr.usgs.gov/htmllib/btch237/btch237j/btch237z/rfl00391.jpg (accessed June 9, 2010).

Figure 13. A typical alluvial fan in the Basin and Range Province. This alluvial fan extends from the Panamint Mountains to the floor of Death Valley in Death Valley National Park, California. These fan-shaped geomorphic features develop as streams flowing from the mouth of steep canyons suddenly encounter the relatively flat topography of the basin margins. Color differences correspond to varying degrees of soil development: lighter colors indicate more recent channel deposits and darker colors indicate older deposits. Photograph by David Miller, U.S. Geological Survey, available online: http://mojave.usgs.gov/rvde/activ_geosoil.html (accessed June 9, 2010).

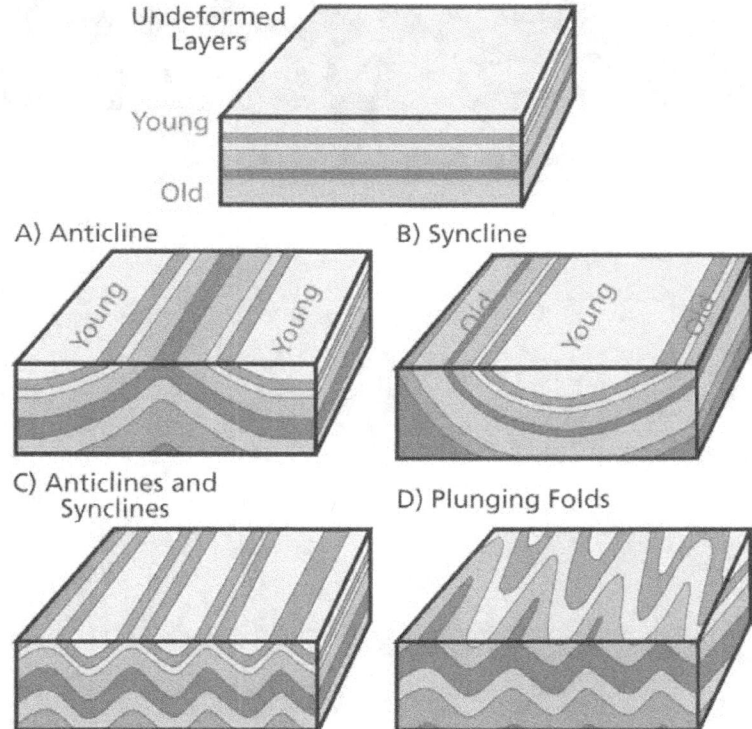

Figure 14. Fold types. A) In an anticline (convex fold), the layers of rock are bent upward. On an eroded surface, the older rocks are exposed in the center of the anticline. B) In a syncline (concave fold), the layers are bent downward, and the younger rocks are exposed in the center of the fold. Diagram modified after Lillie (2005).

Figure 15. San Pedro Valley and the Mule Mountains viewed from the Huachuca Mountains, north of Coronado National Memorial. The graben dropped down along basin-bounding faults (dashed lines) that are now covered by alluvial fan deposits along the margins of the valley. Environmental Protection Agency photograph available online: http://www.epa.gov/nerlesd1/land-sci/san-pedro.htm (accessed March 6, 2010).

Geologic History

This section describes the rocks and unconsolidated deposits that appear on the digital geologic map of Coronado National Memorial, the environment in which those units were deposited, and the timing of geologic events that formed the present landscape.

The rocks and landscape within and surrounding Coronado National Memorial span more than 300 million years of geologic time (figs. 4 and 16). They represent ancient seas, cataclysmic volcanic eruptions, mountain-building, the pulling apart of earth's crust, and recent processes such as debris flows.

Rocks exposed in the southern Huachuca Mountains include Precambrian granite, Paleozoic limestone, Mesozoic igneous and sedimentary rock units, and Cenozoic intrusive rocks. Within Coronado National Memorial, the primary rock types are late Paleozoic limestone and Mesozoic volcanic, granitic, and sedimentary rocks. Pennsylvanian and Permian rocks of the Naco Group (map unit PZl) are the oldest rock units in Coronado National Memorial (fig. 4), and the Cretaceous Morita Formation (map unit Km) is the youngest rock unit (Hon et al. 2007).

Quaternary, Neogene, and Paleocene terrace gravels border the memorial and extend into the San Pedro Valley. Montezuma Canyon contains unconsolidated deposits resulting from debris flows, and cliff collapse has produced talus at the base of steep cliffs in Coronado National Memorial.

Precambrian (prior to 542 million years ago)

The oldest rock in southeastern Arizona is the Pinal Schist, which formed about 1.65 billion years ago during the Precambrian (fig. 16). At that time, the southern shoreline of proto-North America (the ancient core of what is now North America) transected what is now central Arizona, and turbidity currents deposited mud and silt into a marine basin forming offshore. Northwest-directed thrust faulting and folding during the Precambrian Mazatzal Orogeny compressed the basin sediments and attached them to the proto-North American continent (Conway and Silver 1989; Hoffman 1989). Regional metamorphism transformed the sediments into the Pinal Schist. Excellent exposures of Pinal Schist can be found in the Rincon Mountains of Saguaro National Park, east of Tucson, Arizona (Graham 2010).

By 1.4 billion years ago, most of the land surface comprising Arizona had been added to the proto-North American continent. Masses of molten rock then intruded the newly accreted coastal province. The granodiorite in Fort Bowie National Historic Site, for example, intruded the Pinal Schist about 1.375 billion years ago (Drewes 1981, Graham 2011b).

The following 800 million years of geologic history in southeastern Arizona remain a mystery. Erosion has removed any rocks deposited during this time, leaving an unconformity in the geologic record that separates the roughly 1.4-billion-year-old Precambrian rocks from the 510 to 542-million-year-old Cambrian rocks (fig. 16).

Paleozoic Era (542 to 251 million years ago)

Cambrian rocks dating to the beginning of the Paleozoic era record a major oceanic incursion onto the proto-North American continent about 520 million years ago. Southeastern Arizona was covered by an ancient sea during most of the Paleozoic, when thick layers of carbonate and siliceous sediments accumulated on the sea floor.

Undifferentiated units of the Late Paleozoic Naco Group (map unit PZl), which ranges in age from Pennsylvanian (318 to 299 million years ago) to Permian (299 to 251 million years ago), are the only Paleozoic rocks exposed in Coronado National Memorial (fig. 4). In southeastern Arizona, the Naco Group contains seven formations: Pennsylvanian Horquilla Limestone; the Pennsylvanian-to-Permian Earp Formation; the Early Permian Colina Limestone, Epitaph Dolomite, and Scherrer Formation; and the Early- to- Late Permian Concha Limestone and Rainvalley Formation (Blakey and Knepp 1989). Much later, Coronado Cave formed in these undifferentiated Naco Group limestones.

The ledge- and slope-forming Horquilla Limestone (map unit PPNh) crops out throughout southeastern Arizona. In the southern Huachuca Mountains, Pennsylvanian Horquilla Limestone consists of medium-light-gray limestone with interbedded pale-red calcareous siltstone and silty limestone (Hon et al. 2007). Layers of fossiliferous marine limestone and terrigenous mudstone and siltstone record cycles of offshore marine, carbonate-shelf, littoral, and coastal environments, that suggest episodic transgression and regression of the shoreline (Blakey and Knepp 1989).

The Horquilla Limestone transitions gradually into the Earp Formation (map unit PPNe). Contact between these two units is delineated arbitrarily where beds of mudstone and siltstone become predominant over massive limestone beds. The Earp Formation straddles the Pennsylvanian/Permian boundary, and in the southern Huachuca Mountains consists of pale-red calcareous siltstone and mudstone interlayered with thin-bedded limestone and marl. A locally prominent chert-pebble conglomerate forms a thin layer approximately 60 m (200 ft) below the top of the formation. The Pennsylvanian portion of the Earp Formation records shoreline environments that formed when the shallow sea retreated from most of Arizona, and the Permian portion records the return of this sea to southeastern Arizona (Blakey and Knepp 1989).

The calcareous siltstone and mudstone beds of the Earp Formation are gradually replaced by the uniform limestone and dolomite of the Early Permian Colina Limestone (map unit Pc) and Epitaph Dolomite (map unit Pe), mapped in the Sawmill Canyon area northwest of the memorial (Hon et al. 2007). These two rock units formed in different environments at approximately the same time. The medium- to dark-gray Colina Limestone represents deposition on a shallow, clear-water, marine carbonate shelf, and the Epitaph Dolomite formed in restricted marine environments associated with minor local basins (Blakey and Knepp 1989).

In the Early Permian (approximately 290 million years ago), North America was oriented such that the equator ran through Wyoming and eastern Utah on the western margin of Pangaea, the supercontinent that was forming as the globe's landmasses sutured together (fig. 17) (Biek et al. 2000; Morris et al. 2000). The prevalent dry, high-pressure climatic belt in western Pangaea produced restricted marine evaporitic conditions (Peterson 1980).

The dolomite and gypsum in the Epitaph Dolomite record these hot, dry conditions. About 260 m (860 ft) of Epitaph Dolomite forms steep slopes in Sawmill Canyon. A Lower Member consists of about 40 m (130 ft) of medium- and dark-gray to brownish-gray, medium- to thin-bedded dolomite. Gypsum occurs in the Middle Member, along with approximately 140 m (450 ft) of yellowish-gray to pale-pink marl, siltstone, and argillaceous dolomite. Medium- to dark-gray, medium- to thick-bedded resistant dolomite and limestone form the Upper Member (Hon et al. 2007).

In the Huachuca Mountains, up to 53-m (175-ft) of dark-gray Epitaph Dolomite is mapped along with the Colina Limestone, and the upper dolomite interfingers with the base of the overlying Scherrer Formation (map unit Ps). In the southern Huachuca Mountains, the Scherrer Formation consists of a 90-m (300-ft)- thick lower unit of light-brown sandstone and an upper unit of yellowish-gray sandstone that is approximately 30-m (100-ft)-thick. Sandstone in both units is thinly bedded and locally cross-laminated. The base of the formation contains medium-gray dolomite and red mudstone (Hon et al. 2007). Well-sorted quartz sandstone, cross-lamination, and layers of mudstone and dolomite in the Scherrer Formation suggest deposition along a high-energy shoreline in a marine continental-shelf environment.

In the Late Permian, a marine transgression flooded the shoreline, and marine carbonate environments inundated most of Arizona. Cherty, fossiliferous Concha Limestone formed on a broad, shallow, quiet-water, carbonate shelf (Blakey and Knepp 1989). Thin-bedded limestone and interbedded dolomite of the Rainvalley

Formation record the withdrawal of the Permian seas at the end of the Paleozoic.

As the Paleozoic came to a close, subduction of the oceanic plate beneath the proto-North American continent caused west–east thrusting and the addition of continental shelf and slope rocks to the western margin. The South American tectonic plate collided with the proto-North American plate and closed the proto-Gulf of Mexico. This collision caused the uplift of the northwest–southeast-trending Ancestral Rocky Mountains in Colorado, the northeast–southwest-trending Sedona Arch in central Arizona, and the Mogollon Rim uplift in east-central Arizona. South of the Mogollon Rim, an offshore carbonate shelf developed in southeastern Arizona (Blakey 1980; Peterson 1980).

The boundary between the Permian and Triassic periods (and Paleozoic and Mesozoic eras) is marked by the most severe mass extinction event in the last 542 million years. Up to 96% of marine species, including some of those found in the Permian rocks in Coronado National Memorial, and 70% of terrestrial vertebrates may have perished (Raup 1991). The only known mass extinction of insects also occurred at this time. The loss of biodiversity is made apparent by the extinction of 57% of all families and 83% of all genera, including thousands of insect, reptile, and amphibian species and ocean species, such as rugose corals, once-prolific trilobites vanished, snails, urchins, sea lilies (crinoids), and some fish. Five million years later, at the dawn of the Mesozoic era, the chemistry of modern oceans began to evolve and the first mammals and dinosaurs appeared on land.

Mesozoic Era (251 to 65.5 million years ago)
From the middle of the Paleozoic through the Mesozoic, the western margin of North America was an active plate margin where dense oceanic crust subducted beneath lighter continental crust (fig. 18A). Plate convergence generates molten material (magma), primarily from melting in the asthenosphere above the downgoing plate. Magma rises to form plutons and fuel active volcanoes. During the Mesozoic, an arc-shaped belt of volcanic islands, also called a magmatic arc, formed along the western margin of North America (Oldow et al. 1989; Christiansen et al. 1994; Dubiel 1994; Lawton 1994; Peterson 1994). Magma chambers developed, and these igneous intrusions solidified to form plutons and batholiths, such as those exposed in Yosemite National Park, California.

Triassic Period (251 to 200 million years ago)
Thick sections of Triassic rock are present in southern Arizona, but not within Coronado National Memorial. During the Triassic, the supercontinent Pangaea reached its greatest size and was bisected by the equator (Dubiel 1994). Thereafter, Pangaea began to split apart.

The Triassic development of a northwest-flowing fluvial system in the southwestern United States included north-flowing tributaries in southern Arizona (Dubiel 1994). The Late Triassic was an unusually wet time period for the western interior of North America, and principal depositional environments included fluvial, floodplain, marsh, and lacustrine settings. Minor eolian and playa environments formed at the close of the Triassic.

Jurassic Period (200 to 145 million years ago)

Dramatic modifications to the western margin of North America occurred in the Jurassic. The thick sequence of Late Triassic and Jurassic continental volcanic rocks in southeastern Arizona represents a major change from the shallow marine shelf conditions that persisted in the region during most of the Paleozoic (Kluth 1983; Dubiel 1994; Peterson 1994). Oblique subduction of the oceanic plate beneath the overriding North American plate created a northwest-trending volcanic arc along the southwestern margin of North America (Tosdal et al. 1989).

In the Early Jurassic (200 to 176 million years ago), voluminous pyroclastic rocks and volcanic flows erupted across most of the Sonoran Desert region of Arizona (fig. 3). Crustal extension occurred locally within the volcanic arc. Quartz-rich eolian sand blew into the region from extensive dune fields located on the southern Colorado Plateau (Bilodeau et al. 1987; Tosdal et al. 1989). For approximately 35 million years, into the Middle and perhaps early Late Jurassic, explosive volcanism dramatically modified the southern Arizona landscape.

In the Middle Jurassic (176 to 161 million years ago), Wrangellia, a collection of islands in the Pacific, collided with North America, causing volcanic activity along the west coast from Mexico to Canada (fig. 19). The collision caused west-east thrust faulting in Nevada. A shallow sea encroached into Utah from the north. About 165 million years ago, catastrophic volcanic eruptions in southeastern Arizona formed calderas in the Huachuca and southern Dragoon mountains.

Volcanic deposits from three overlapping caldera complexes are present in the Coronado National Memorial area (Hon and Lipman 1994). Lava, megabreccia, and dacitic ash-flow tuff from the Montezuma Caldera are the oldest deposits (map units Jmb, Jhl). After the Montezuma Caldera collapsed, Huachuca granite (map units Jh) intruded into the tuff.

Following the emplacement of Huachuca granite, a phenocryst-poor rhyolite tuff (map unit Jrt) erupted from the Turkey Canyon Caldera northwest of the memorial. Located in the Turkey Canyon area of the Canelo Hills, the caldera occupies an elliptical area about 6 km (3.7 mi) long (Lipman and Hagstrum 1992). Exposures of igneous intrusions similar to those associated with the Montezuma Caldera have not been found in association with the Turkey Canyon Caldera.

The youngest of the three calderas, the Parker Canyon Caldera, erupted in the Canelo Hills and produced a phenocryst-rich rhyolite tuff (map unit Jpt). Like the other two calderas, the Parker Canyon Caldera contains megablocks of limestone and landslide material. A quartz-rich, post-caldera intrusion is exposed in lower Parker Canyon (Lipman and Hagstrum 1992).

Sediments separating the three ash-flow tuffs indicate the passage of time between caldera-forming events (map unit Jqlt). Similar amounts of sediment found within Paleogene calderas took tens of thousands to hundreds of thousands of years to accumulate (Hon and Lipman 1994).

By the mid-Late Jurassic, strike-slip faulting (fig. 5) related to the opening of the Gulf of Mexico generated large-scale, high-angle, primarily northwest-trending faults in southern Arizona (Tosdal et al. 1989). A large strike-slip fault zone, the Mojave-Sonora megashear, truncated the southwestern continental margin of North America (Kluth 1983; Anderson and Silver 2005; Stevens et al. 2005). The northwest–southeast-trending megashear accommodated approximately 800 to 1,000 km (500 to 600 mi) of displacement (Anderson and Silver 2005; Haenggi and Muehlberger 2005).

The widespread Jurassic ash-flow deposits and calderas in southeastern Arizona support the interpretation that this area underwent regional extension during the Jurassic. The ash-flows constitute a volcanic suite dominated by light-colored felsic rocks (rhyolite), with smaller volumes of dark-colored mafic rocks (andesite, basalt). The chemical composition of the mafic rocks is similar to that of chemical features associated with known regions of tectonic extension (Lipman and Hagstrum 1992).

At the end of the Jurassic, the production and movement of magma (magmatism) waned and finally ended. Rift (pull-apart) tectonics formed the Bisbee trough that extended into southeastern Arizona from the Gulf of Mexico. Alluvial-fan and fluvial deposits of the Bisbee Group (Glance Conglomerate) accumulated in the depression (Tosdal et al. 1989; Elder and Kirkland 1994; Dickinson and Lawton 2001; Haenggi and Muehlberger 2005).

Cretaceous Period (145 to 65.5 million years ago)

During the Early Cretaceous (145 to 100 million years ago) in southern Arizona, rifting along the northwest–southeast-trending Bisbee basin dominated the tectonic regime. Rifting associated with the Mojave-Sonora megashear opened a series of local pull-apart basins (Elder and Kirkland 1994; Anderson and Nourse 2005).

The Glance Conglomerate (map unit Jg), the basal unit of the Lower-Cretaceous Bisbee Group in southern Arizona, represents proximal deposits of alluvial-fan systems that rimmed local fault-block mountain ranges and the Bisbee basin (Bilodeau 1982; Bilodeau et al. 1987; Dickinson et al. 1987; Lipman and Hagstrum 1992). At Coronado National Memorial, the chaotic landslide breccia in the Glance Conglomerate suggests seismic activity and possibly a resurgent dome associated with the Montezuma Caldera (Bilodeau et al. 1987). Fluvial and floodplain deposits in the Morita Formation (Bisbee Group) represent continued deposition on a slowly subsiding deltaic plain (Hayes 1970).

The Mogollon highlands flanked the Bisbee basin to the north, and an emergent area associated with the active magmatic arc lay to the southwest (Dickinson et al. 1989). The fossiliferous Mural Limestone (not exposed in the memorial), which overlies the Morita Formation (map unit Km), marks the maximum marine transgression within the Bisbee basin (Dickinson et al. 1989).

Approximately 90 million years ago, early in the Late Cretaceous, oceanic–continental plate convergence along the western margin of North America during the Sevier Orogeny caused sedimentary strata to be folded and thrust eastward over Precambrian basement rocks. The rising mountains in the fold-and-thrust belt extended from Canada to Mexico. Sediment eroded from the mountains was deposited in an adjacent foreland basin that formed landward of the mountain range. Rifting of the Gulf of Mexico continued to the south caused seawater to encroach northward into the subsiding basin. Marine water also began to transgress southward from the Arctic region. The seas advanced and retreated many times during the Cretaceous until a seaway extended from today's Gulf of Mexico to the Arctic Ocean, a distance of about 5,000 km (3,000 mi) (Kauffman 1977). Southeastern Arizona formed part of the western border of this Western Interior Seaway, the most extensive interior seaway ever recorded in North America (fig. 20).

With the advent of the Laramide Orogeny, approximately 75 million years ago, the Western Interior Seaway began to retreat from the continent. The subducting slab was relatively flat during the Laramide Orogeny, in contrast to the steep subduction angle thought to be responsible for the Sevier Orogeny (fig. 18B). Because flat-slab subduction transferred the compressive stress farther inland, the Laramide Orogeny displaced deep-seated basement blocks of Precambrian rocks. Reverse and thrust faults transported these Precambrian units to the surface, and they are now exposed in the Rocky Mountains.

In southern Arizona, nonmarine strata of the Fort Crittenden Formation (exposed in the Huachuca Mountains but not in Coronado National Memorial) record the initial advance of the Laramide Orogeny into the area (Hayes 1987, 1988). Composed primarily of conglomeratic alluvial-fan and braided-stream deposits, the formation contains abundant volcaniclastic debris and some minor lacustrine mudstones (Dickinson et al. 1989).

At the close of the Mesozoic Era about 65 million years ago, the Laramide Orogeny caused another burst of volcanic activity and faulting in southeastern Arizona. The Laramide Orogeny, which lasted until approximately 35 million years ago, is responsible for the

creation of the modern Rocky Mountains and for the deposition of most copper, silver, and gold ores in the southwestern United States, including those in the southern Huachuca Mountains and Coronado National Memorial (Pallister et al. 1997).

Cenozoic Era (65.5 million years ago to present)

Paleogene and Neogene (65.5 to 2.6 million years ago)

Two processes dominated tectonic evolution and sedimentation in Arizona during this period: the resurgence of magma production and movement after a 10- to- 30-million-year quiescence, and lithospheric extension that gave rise to the present basin-and-range topography (Spencer and Reynolds 1989). Both processes were related to the evolving plate-tectonic setting of the western continental margin of North America. The Laramide Orogeny ended as the angle of subduction increased along the western margin in the Paleogene. Compressive forces decreased in the interior of western North America, allowing normal extensional faults (normal faults) to develop.

Multiple plutonic intrusions occurred in southern Arizona in the Paleogene and early Miocene (fig. 16). Near Tucson, Arizona, the Santa Catalina Mountains contain at least 12 plutons recording three intrusive episodes: 1) 60 to 75 million years ago (Latest Cretaceous to Paleocene), 2) 44 to 50 million years ago (Eocene), and 3) 25 to 29 million years ago (Oligocene) (Anderson 1988).

Volcanic activity returned to southeastern Arizona during the second of these intrusive episodes (40 to 45 million years ago). Lavas and low-volume tuffs erupted from a series of volcanic vents (Dickinson 1979; Nations et al. 1985; Kring 2002). A large number of volcanic calderas subsequently formed in southern Arizona and New Mexico, including the Oligocene-aged (26.9 million years ago) Turkey Creek Caldera, that deposited most of the volcanic rocks in Chiricahua National Monument, northeast of Coronado National Memorial. This caldera is about 19 km (12 mi) in diameter (Drewes 1982; Kring 2002; Graham 2009).

Beginning about 15 to 10 million years ago (Miocene), lithospheric extension began shaping the present basin-and-range topography (figs. 3 and 6). The crust broke into blocks separated by new, more steeply dipping faults. Some blocks were displaced by as much as 1.4 km (2.4 mi) relative to other blocks to form deep grabens, such as the San Pedro graben. In the upper San Pedro Valley adjacent to Coronado National Memorial, most basin-fill sediments range from 250 to 350 m (820 to 1,150 ft) thick, but can locally exceed 1,000 m (3,300 ft) in thickness (Gettings and Houser 2000).

Some basin-and-range normal faults dipped gently beneath Earth's surface, forming detachment (décollement) faults that caused up to 10 to 25 km (6 to 15 mi) of separation between formerly proximate regions. During fault movement, deeply buried rocks beneath the fault began to rise to the surface as the confining pressure of the overlying rocks was removed. These rising rocks were composed primarily of metamorphic mineral assemblages formed at unusually high temperatures and pressures. They are exposed at the surface as dome-shaped mountain ranges called metamorphic core complexes.

More than 25 of these distinctive, isolated, domed mountain ranges extend in a narrow sinuous belt from southern Canada to northwestern Mexico (Coney 1979; Davis 1987; Spencer and Reynolds 1989; Dickinson 1991). The Rincon Mountain District of Saguaro National Park forms part of a metamorphic core complex that includes the Tortilita, Santa Catalina, and Rincon mountains (Graham 2010). No metamorphic core complexes are exposed in Coronado National Memorial.

Quaternary Period (2.6 million years ago to present)

Quaternary tectonic activity (tectonism) has been a minor influence in most areas of the Mexican Highland section of the Basin and Range Province (fig. 3). Mountain peaks (e.g., Bob Thompson, Montezuma peaks), and ranges (e.g., Huachuca Mountains) are generally higher, longer, and more closely spaced in the Mexican Highland section than in the Sonoran Desert to the west (Morrison 1991). Intermontane basin floors are also higher than in the Sonoran Desert, and all but two of the basins (Hualapai, central Sulfur Spring valleys) contain external drainage.

At the beginning of the Pliocene (approximately 5 million years ago), the frequency and severity of basin-and-range deformation began to decrease (fig. 16). Erosion and sedimentation were increasingly controlled by climate, rather than by tectonism (Menges and Pearthree 1989; Morrison 1991). In the early Pleistocene, the southern Arizona climate was generally uniform, warm, and semiarid. Erosion and deposition rates decreased dramatically in comparison with what they had been during Neogene basin-and-range deformation. Fluvial deposits in the basins were finer-grained than previously, and paleosols (ancient soils) had time to develop on alluvial surfaces. This period of relative tectonic and climatic quiescence produced extensive pediments throughout the Mexican Highland section (Morrison 1991). Common in arid and semiarid regions, pediments

are broad, rock-floored erosion surfaces that slope gently from the base of an abrupt and retreating mountain front.

Exposures of Pliocene and Quaternary sedimentary sequences in the Mexican Highland section of Arizona record deposition within internally-drained basins throughout the Pliocene and early Pleistocene. Thick sequences of gravel and sand grade to silt, clay, marl, and other lake sediments in the basin interiors (Morrison 1991).

Climatic oscillations increased throughout the early Pleistocene in a pattern consistent with the evolution of global climate change during the Pleistocene ice ages (fig. 21). Erosional unconformities and changes in sediment amount and particle size record an increase in precipitation and runoff and an end to the relative landscape stability of the Pliocene and early Pleistocene. The development of through-going drainage systems connected adjacent, formerly internally drained basins. This establishment of exterior drainage led to the formation of through-going streams, rather than lakes in basin interiors. Episodes of vertical downcutting punctuated by episodes of lateral erosion resulted in stepped series of stream terraces, such as those along the eastern border of Coronado National Memorial ("Qg" map units).

Narrow modern washes along active stream channels contain Late Pleistocene and Holocene alluvial deposits of silt, sand, and gravel. Recent gravels may also be transported onto alluvial fans by seasonal floods. These undeformed, unconsolidated deposits overlap the San Pedro basin-boundary fault (Morrison 1991; Hon et al. 2007).

Today, erosion and weathering processes continue to wear down the Huachuca Mountains. Unconsolidated talus deposits (map unit Qt) reflect recent cliff collapse in the canyons, and localized deposits of clay-to-boulder-sized material in Montezuma Canyon record Holocene debris-flow events (map unit Qd). The 2006 and 2008 debris flows are evidence of this continuing geologic process.

Eon	Era	Period	Epoch	Ma	Life Forms	North American Events
Phanerozoic	Cenozoic	Quaternary	Holocene	0.01	Modern humans *(Age of Mammals)*	Cascade volcanoes (W)
			Pleistocene		Extinction of large mammals and birds	Worldwide glaciation
		Neogene (Tertiary)	Pliocene	2.6	Large carnivores	Sierra Nevada Mountains (W)
			Miocene	5.3	Whales and apes	Linking of North and South America
			Oligocene	23.0		Basin-and-Range extension (W)
		Paleogene (Tertiary)	Eocene	33.9		
			Paleocene	55.8	Early primates	Laramide Orogeny ends (W)
				65.5		
	Mesozoic	Cretaceous			Mass extinction *(Age of Dinosaurs)*	Laramide Orogeny (W)
					Placental mammals	Sevier Orogeny (W)
				145.5	Early flowering plants	Nevadan Orogeny (W)
		Jurassic			First mammals	Elko Orogeny (W)
				199.6	Mass extinction	Breakup of Pangaea begins
		Triassic			Flying reptiles First dinosaurs	Sonoma Orogeny (W)
	Paleozoic	Permian		251	Mass extinction *(Age of Amphibians)* Coal-forming forests diminish	Supercontinent Pangaea intact Ouachita Orogeny (S) Alleghanian (Appalachian) Orogeny (E)
		Pennsylvanian		299	Coal-forming swamps Sharks abundant	Ancestral Rocky Mountains (W)
		Mississippian		318.1	Variety of insects First amphibians	
		Devonian		359.2	First reptiles Mass extinction *(Fishes)* First forests (evergreens)	Antler Orogeny (W) Acadian Orogeny (E-NE)
		Silurian		416	First land plants	
		Ordovician		443.7	Mass extinction First primitive fish Trilobite maximum Rise of corals	Taconic Orogeny (E-NE)
		Cambrian		488.3	Early shelled organisms *(Marine Invertebrates)*	Avalonian Orogeny (NE) Extensive oceans cover most of proto-North America (Laurentia)
				542		
Proterozoic		Precambrian			First multicelled organisms	Supercontinent rifted apart Formation of early supercontinent Grenville Orogeny (E)
				2500	Jellyfish fossil (670 Ma)	First iron deposits Abundant carbonate rocks
Archean				≈4000	Early bacteria and algae	Oldest known Earth rocks (≈3.96 billion years ago)
Hadean					Origin of life?	Oldest moon rocks (4–4.6 billion years ago)
				4600	Formation of the Earth	Formation of Earth's crust

Figure 16. Geologic timescale. Included are major life history and tectonic events occurring on the North American continent. Red lines indicate major unconformities between eras. Radiometric ages shown are in millions of years (Ma). Compass directions in parentheses indicate the regional location of individual geologic events. Graphic by Trista Thornberry-Ehrlich (Colorado State University) with information from the U.S. Geological Survey (http://pubs.usgs.gov/fs/2007/3015/) with additional information from the International Commission on Stratigraphy (http://www.stratigraphy.org/view.php?id=25).

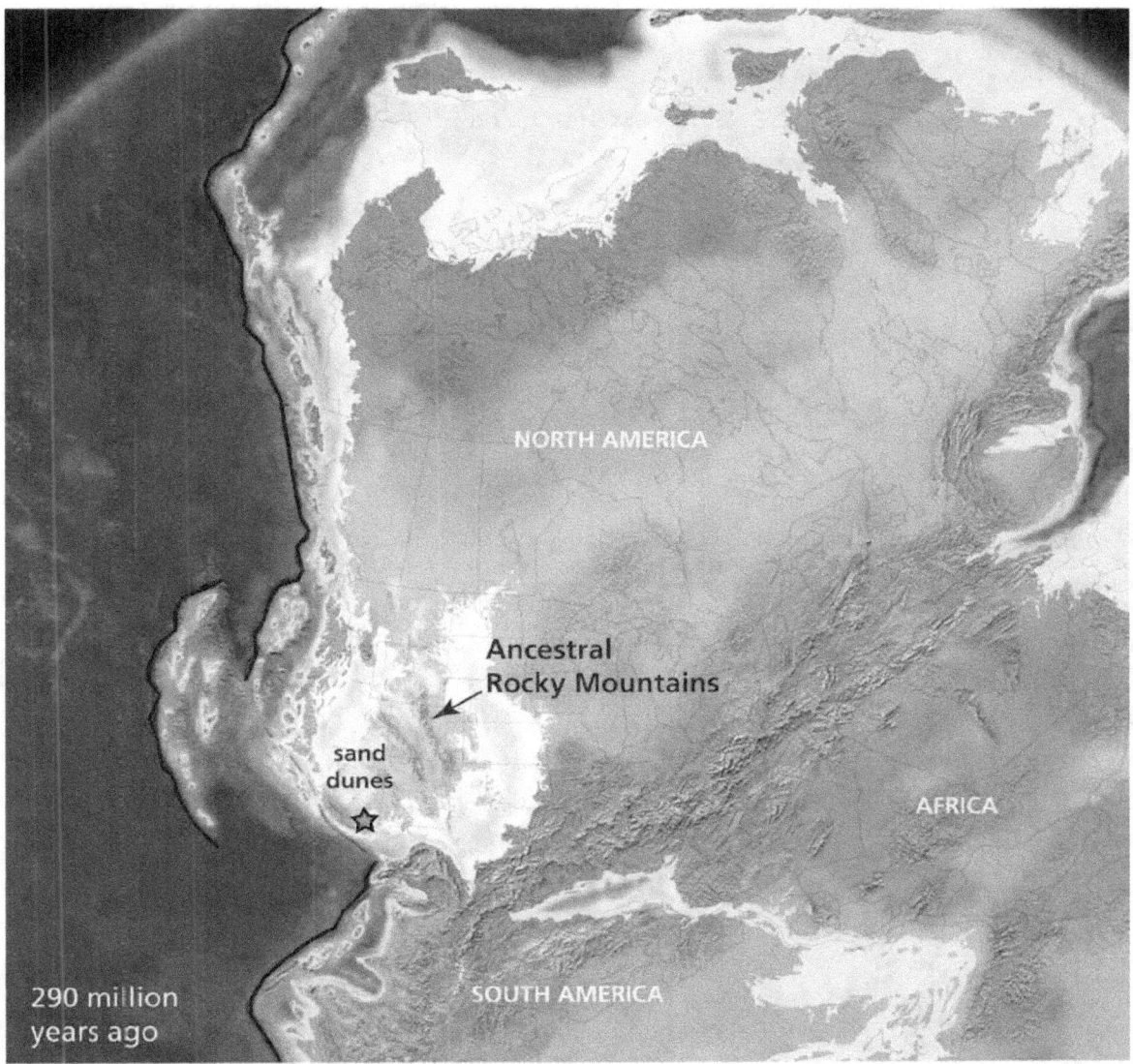

Figure 17. Early Permian (290 million years ago) paleogeographic map of North America. Remnants of the northwest–southeast-trending Ancestral Rocky Mountains (dark brown) can still be seen in Colorado. The light-brown color in northeastern and central Arizona represents sand deposited in an arid dune environment. Marine basins in southeastern Arizona and southwestern New Mexico are closing as proto-South America collides with proto-North America. Thick black lines mark the location of the subduction zone off the western margin of the land mass that will soon become the supercontinent Pangaea. The green star represents the approximate location of present-day Coronado National Memorial. Brown colors indicate land surface. Relative depths of marine water are indicated by light-blue (shallow) and dark-blue (deep) colors. Base paleogeographic map by Ron Blakey, Colorado Plateau Geosystems, Inc., available online: http://cpgeosystems.com/namP290.jpg, accessed June 9, 2010. Annotation by the author.

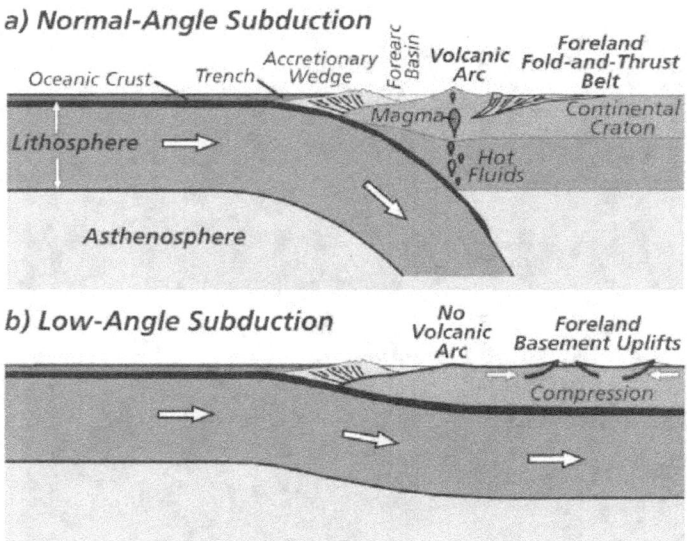

a) Normal-Angle Subduction

b) Low-Angle Subduction

Figure 18. Normal-angle and low-angle subduction diagrams. A) In a normal plate-tectonic setting, a relatively steep angle of subduction causes melting above the downgoing slab. Magma rises to the surface and erupts, forming a chain of volcanoes (volcanic arc) along the continental margin, similar to the present Andes Mountains of South America. Sedimentary strata are folded and thrust toward the continental craton in a "foreland fold-and-thrust belt."In the Triassic, oceanic-oceanic plate convergence caused the volcanic arc to form offshore. During the Jurassic, the oceanic plate collided with the North American continent and the volcanic arc formed along the western margin of North America, as depicted in this diagram. B) During the Laramide Orogeny, the subducting slab flattened out, and deformation occurred farther inland. The downgoing slab in low-angle subduction does not extend deep enough to heat up and produce magma so volcanism ceases or migrates toward the craton. The subducting slab transmits stress farther inland, causing hard rock in the crust to compress and break along reverse faults, forming basement uplifts such as those in today's Rocky Mountains. Diagram from Lillie (2005), courtesy Robert J. Lillie (Oregon State University).

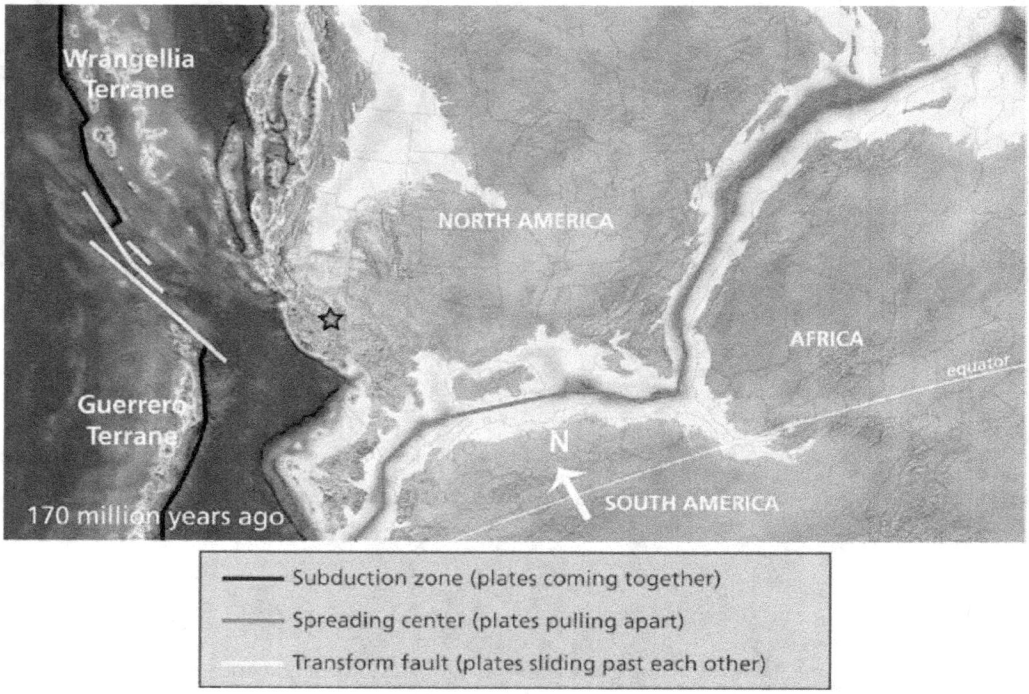

Figure 19. Middle Jurassic paleogeographic map of the southern half of the North American continent. Approximately 170 million years ago, the Greater Wrangellia Terrane collided with North America, forming a string of active volcanoes from Mexico to Canada along the western and causing thrust faulting in Nevada. The volcanic arc in the Wrangellia Terrane included the present-day Wrangell Mountains, the Queen Charlotte Islands, and Vancouver Island. The Guerrero Terrane closed to the south. The green star approximates the location of present-day Coronado National Memorial. A foreland basin formed landward of the thrusting in Nevada and allowed an epicontinental sea to encroach from the north. South America and Africa are rifting away from North America. The white line indicates the Middle Jurassic equator. Brown colors indicate land surface. Relative depths of marine water are indicated by light-blue (shallow) and dark-blue (deep) colors. Base paleogeographic map by Ron Blakey, Colorado Plateau Geosystems, Inc., available online: http://cpgeosystems.com/namJ170.jpg, accessed June 9, 2010. Annotation by the author.

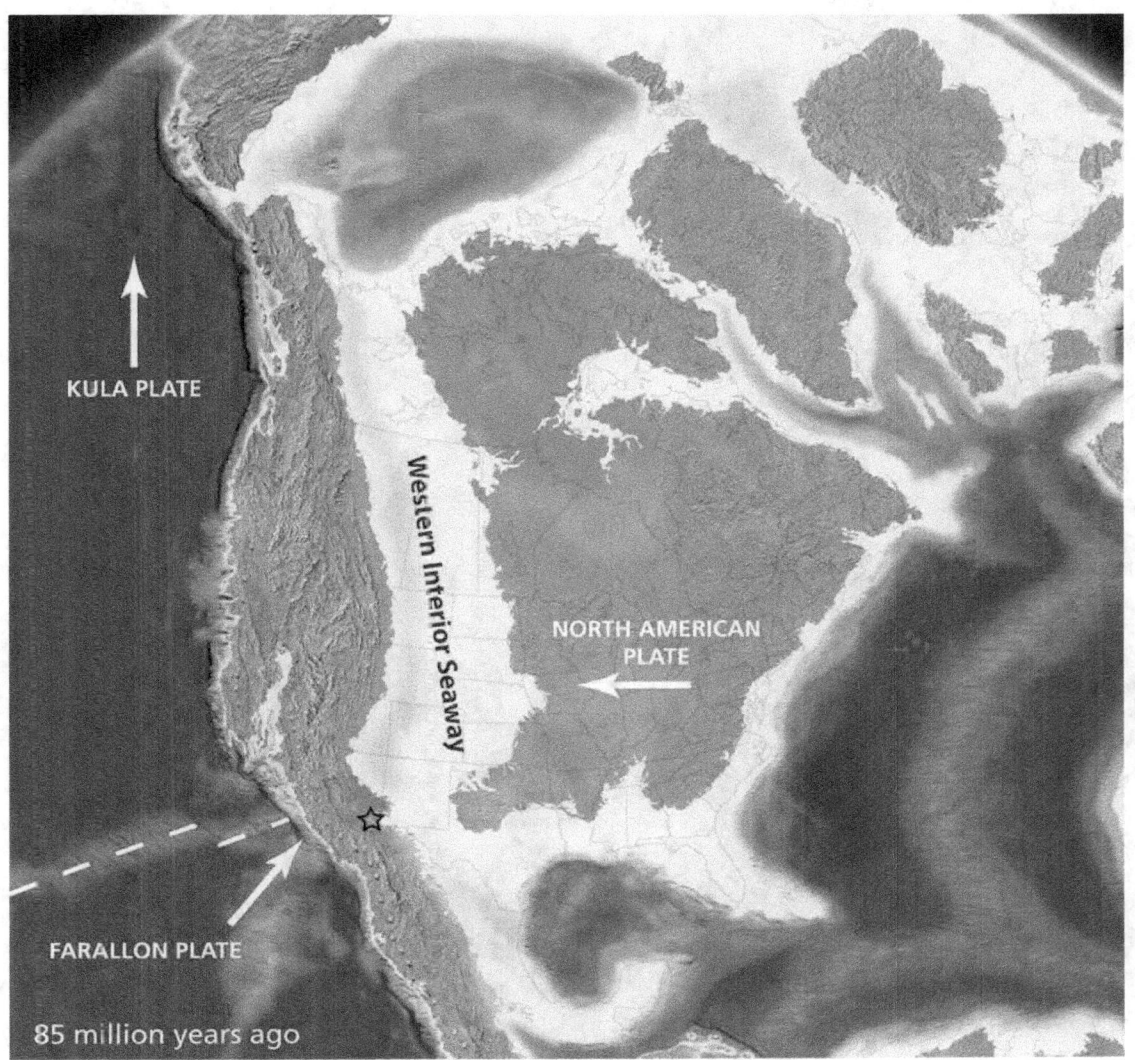

Figure 20. Late Cretaceous paleogeographic map of North America. Approximately 85 million years ago, the Western Interior Seaway reached its maximum extent. The Sevier Orogeny produced fold-and-thrust-belt mountains along the western continental margin. Regional metamorphism affected western Arizona and eastern California. Paleozoic and Mesozoic sandstone, mudstone, and limestone were metamorphosed to quartzite, schist, and marble. The green star marks the approximate location of present-day Coronado National Memorial. Arrows indicate the general direction of plate movement. Brown colors indicate land surface. Relative depths of marine water are indicated by light-blue (shallow) and dark-blue (deep) colors. Base paleogeographic map by Ron Blakey, Colorado Plateau Geosystems, Inc., available online: http://cpgeosystems.com/namK85.jpg, accessed June 9, 2010. Annotation by the author.

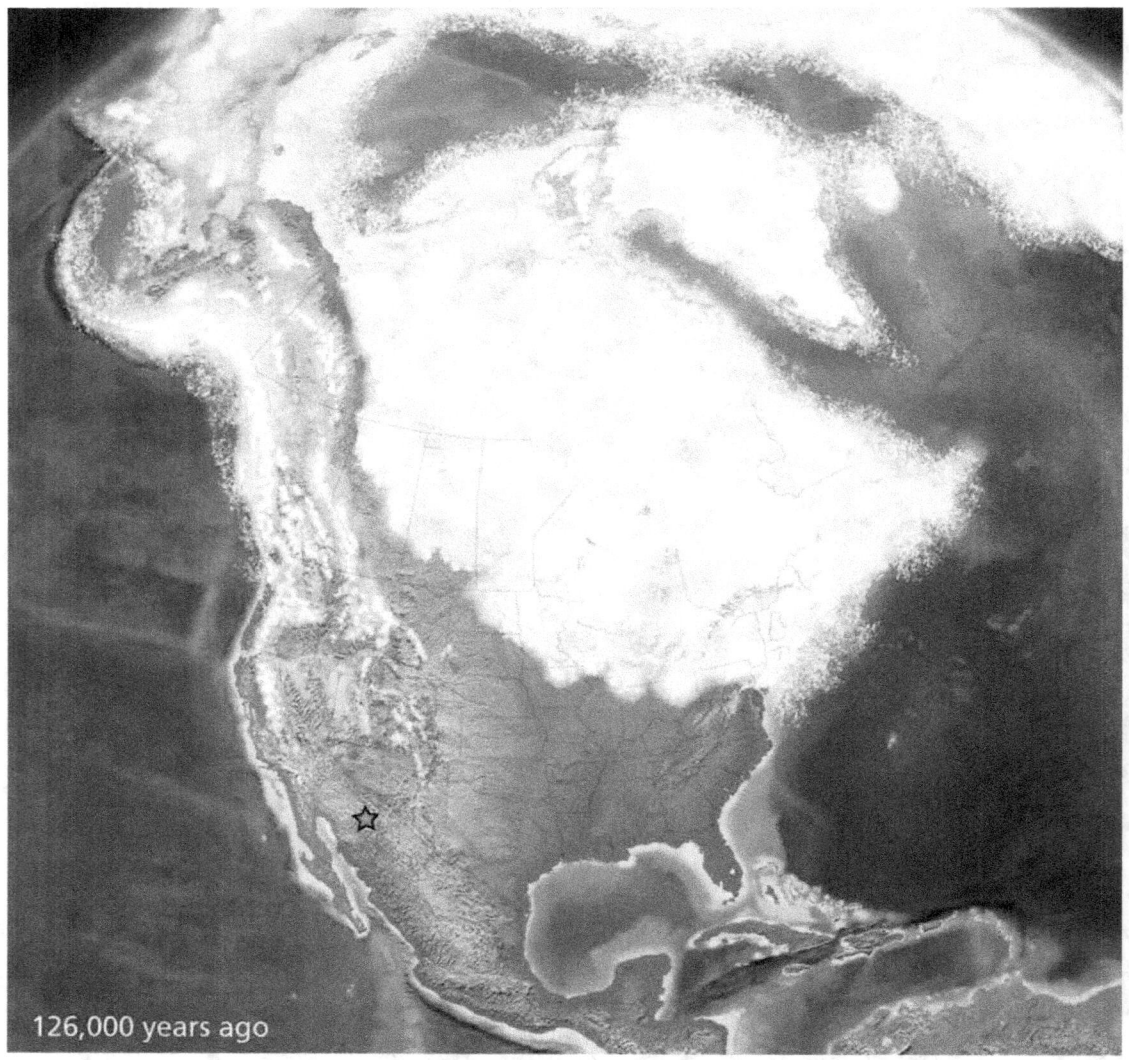

126,000 years ago

Figure 21. Paleogeographic map of North America during the Pleistocene epoch. Approximately 126,000 years ago, global climatic oscillations caused continental ice sheets to migrate into northern North America and alpine glaciers to form in western and southern mountainous areas. Green star approximates the location of present-day Coronado National Memorial. Base paleogeographic map by Ron Blakey, Colorado Plateau Geosystems, Inc., available online: http://cpgeosystems.com/namQ.jpg, accessed June 9, 2010. Annotation by the author.

Geologic Map Data

This section summarizes the geologic map data available for Coronado National Memorial. It includes a fold-out geologic map overview and a summary table that lists each map unit displayed on the digital geologic map for the park. Complete GIS data are included on the accompanying CD and are also available at the Geologic Resources Inventory (GRI) publications website: http://www.nature.nps.gov/geology/ inventory/gre_publications.cfm.

Geologic Maps

Geologic maps facilitate an understanding of an area's geologic framework and the evolution of its present landscape. Using designated colors and symbols, geologic maps portray the spatial distribution and relationships of rocks and unconsolidated deposits. Geologic maps also may show geomorphic features, structural interpretations, and locations of past geologic hazards that may be prone to future activity. Additionally, anthropogenic features such as mines and quarries may be indicated on geologic maps.

Source Maps

The Geologic Resources Inventory (GRI) team converts digital and/or paper source maps into the GIS formats that conform to the GRI GIS data model. The GRI digital geologic map product also includes essential elements of the source maps including unit descriptions, map legend, map notes, references, and figures. The GRI team used the following source maps to create the digital geologic data for Coronado National Memorial:

Hon, K. A., F. Gray, K. S. Bolm, K. A. Dempsey, and P. A. Pearthree. 2007. A digital geologic map of the Miller Peak, Nicksville, Bob Thompson Peak, and Montezuma Pass Quadrangles, Arizona. U.S. Geological Survey Scientific Investigations Map, SIM unpublished (scale 1:24,000).

This source map provided information for the "Geologic Issues," "Geologic Features and Processes," and "Geologic History" sections of this report.

Geologic GIS Data

The GRI team implements a GIS data model that standardizes map deliverables. The data model is included on the enclosed CD and is also available online (http://science.nature.nps.gov/im/inventory/geology /GeologyGISDataModel.cfm). This data model dictates GIS data structure including layer architecture, feature attribution, and relationships within ESRI ArcGIS software. The GRI team digitized the data for Coronado National Memorial using data model version 2.0.

GRI digital geologic data for Coronado National Memorial are included on the attached CD and are available through the NPS Integrated Resource Management Applications (IRMA) (https://irma.nps.gov/App/Reference/Search? SearchType=Q). Enter "GRI" as the search text and select the park from the unit list. Note that as of September 2011, IRMA is only compatible with the Internet Explorer browser. The following components and geology data layers are part of the data set:

- Data in ESRI geodatabase and shapefile GIS formats
- Layer files with feature symbology
- Federal Geographic Data Committee (FGDC)– compliant metadata
- A PDF document (coro_geology.pdf) that contains all of the ancillary map information and graphics, including geologic unit correlation tables and map unit descriptions, legends, and other information captured from source maps.
- An ESRI map document file (coro_geology.mxd) that displays the digital geologic data

Table 2. Geology data layers in the Coronado National Memorial GIS data.

Data Layer	Code	On Geologic Map Overview?
Geologic Attitude Observation Points	coroatd	No
Mine Point Features	coromin	No
Fault and Fold Map Symbology	corosym	Yes
Folds	corofld	Yes
Faults	coroflt	Yes
Linear Dikes	corodke	Yes
Geologic Contacts	coroglga	Yes
Geologic Units	coroglg	Yes

Note: All data layers may not be visible on the geologic map overview graphic.

Geologic Map Overview

The fold-out geologic map overview displays the GRI digital geologic data draped over a shaded relief image of Coronado National Memorial and includes basic geographic information. For graphic clarity and legibility, not all GIS feature classes are visible on the overview. The digital elevation data and geographic information are not included with the GRI digital geologic GIS data for the park, but are available online from a variety of sources.

Map Unit Properties Table

The geologic units listed in the fold-out map unit properties table correspond to the accompanying digital geologic data. In addition to geologic descriptions of each unit, the table highlights resource management considerations for each unit. The units, their relationships, and the series of events the created them are highlighted in the "Geologic History" section. Please refer to the geologic timescale (fig. 16) for the geologic period and age associated with each unit.

Use Constraints

Graphic and written information provided in this section is not a substitute for site-specific investigations, and ground-disturbing activities should neither be permitted nor denied based upon the information provided here. Minor inaccuracies may exist regarding the location of geologic features relative to other geologic or geographic features on the overview graphic. Based on the source map scale (1:24,000) and U.S. National Map Accuracy Standards, geologic features represented here are within 12 meters / 40 feet (horizontally) of their true location.

Please contact GRI with any questions.

Overview of Digital Geologic Data
for Coronado National Memorial

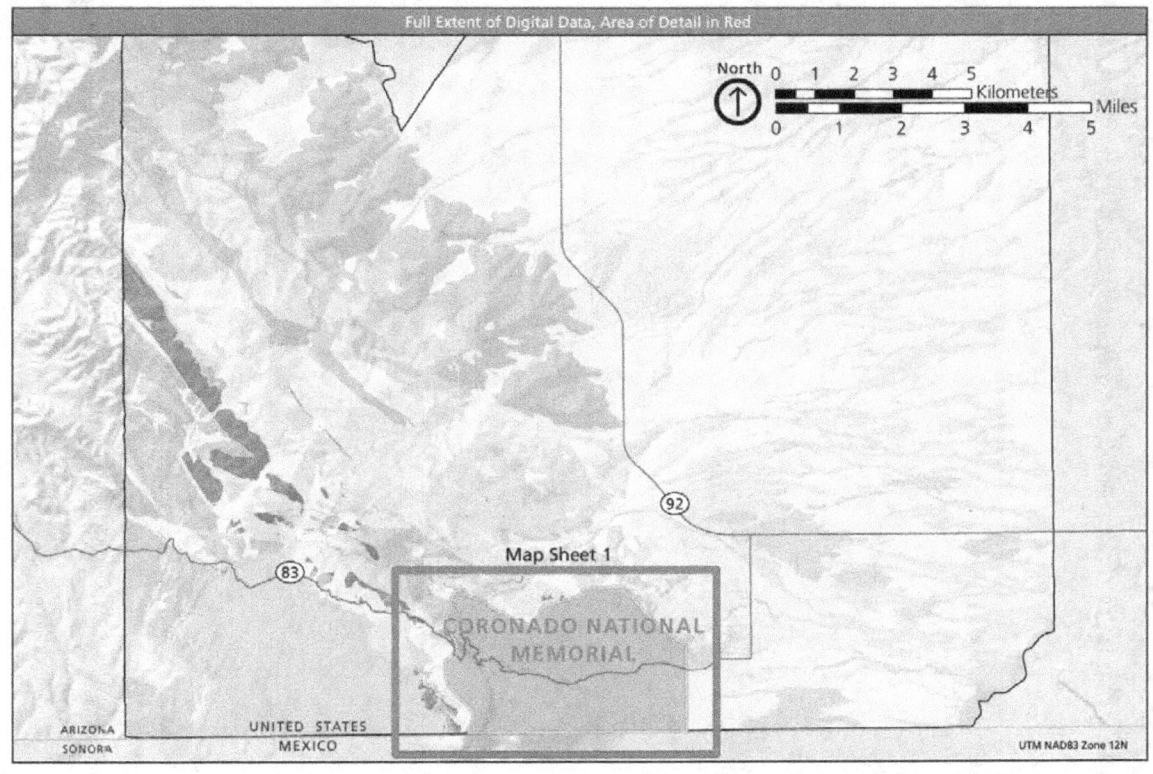

Full Extent of Digital Data, Area of Detail in Red

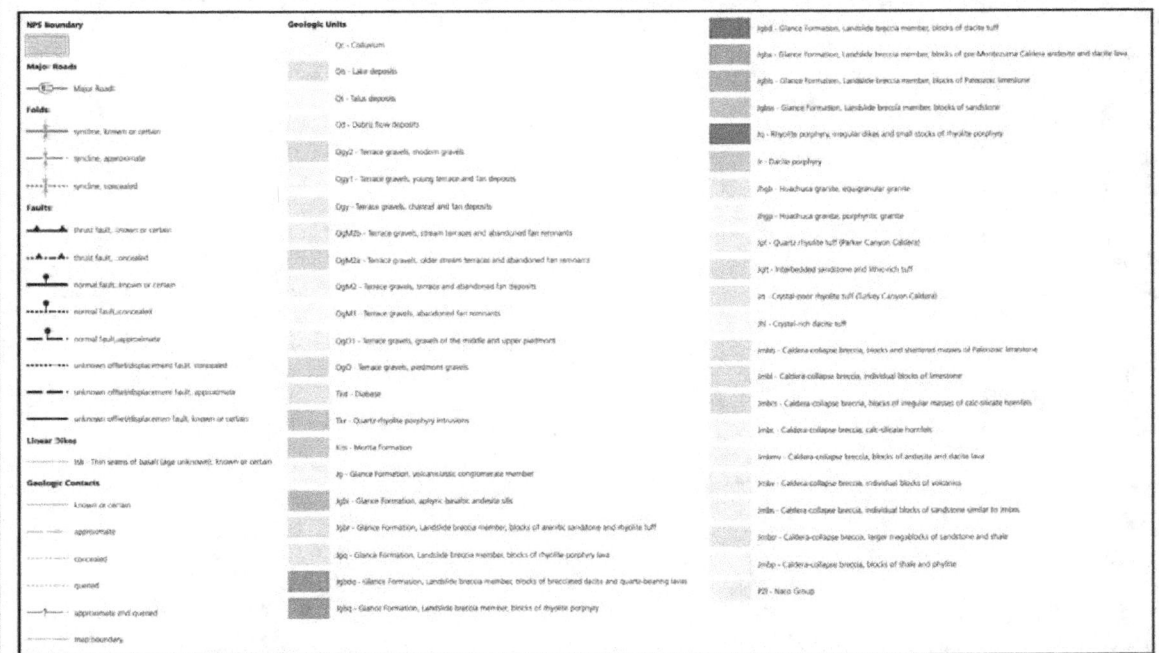

This figure is an overview of compiled digital geologic data. It is not a substitute for site-specific investigations.

Minor inaccuracies may exist regarding the location of geologic features relative to other geologic or geographic features on the figure. Based on the source map scale (1:24,000) and U.S. National Map Accuracy Standards, geologic features represented here are within 12 meters /40 feet (horizontally) of their true location.

This figure was prepared as part of the NPS Geologic Resources Division's Geologic Resources Inventory. The source map used in creation of the digital geologic data product was:

Hon, K. A., F. Gray, K. F. Bolm, K. A. Dempsey, and P. A. Pearthree. 2007. A Digital Geologic Map of the Miller Peak, Nicksville, Bob Thompson Peak, and Montezuma Pass Quadrangles, Arizona (scale 1:24,000 scale). Scientific Investigations Map, unpublished. U.S. Geological Survey

Digital geologic data and cross sections for Coronado National Memorial, and all other digital geologic data prepared as part of the Geologic Resources Inventory, are available online at the NPS Natural Resource Information Portal https://nrinfo.nps.gov/Reference.mvc/Search. (Enter "GRI" as the search textand select Coronado National Memorial from the unit list.)

Overview of Digital Geologic Data for Coronado National Memorial

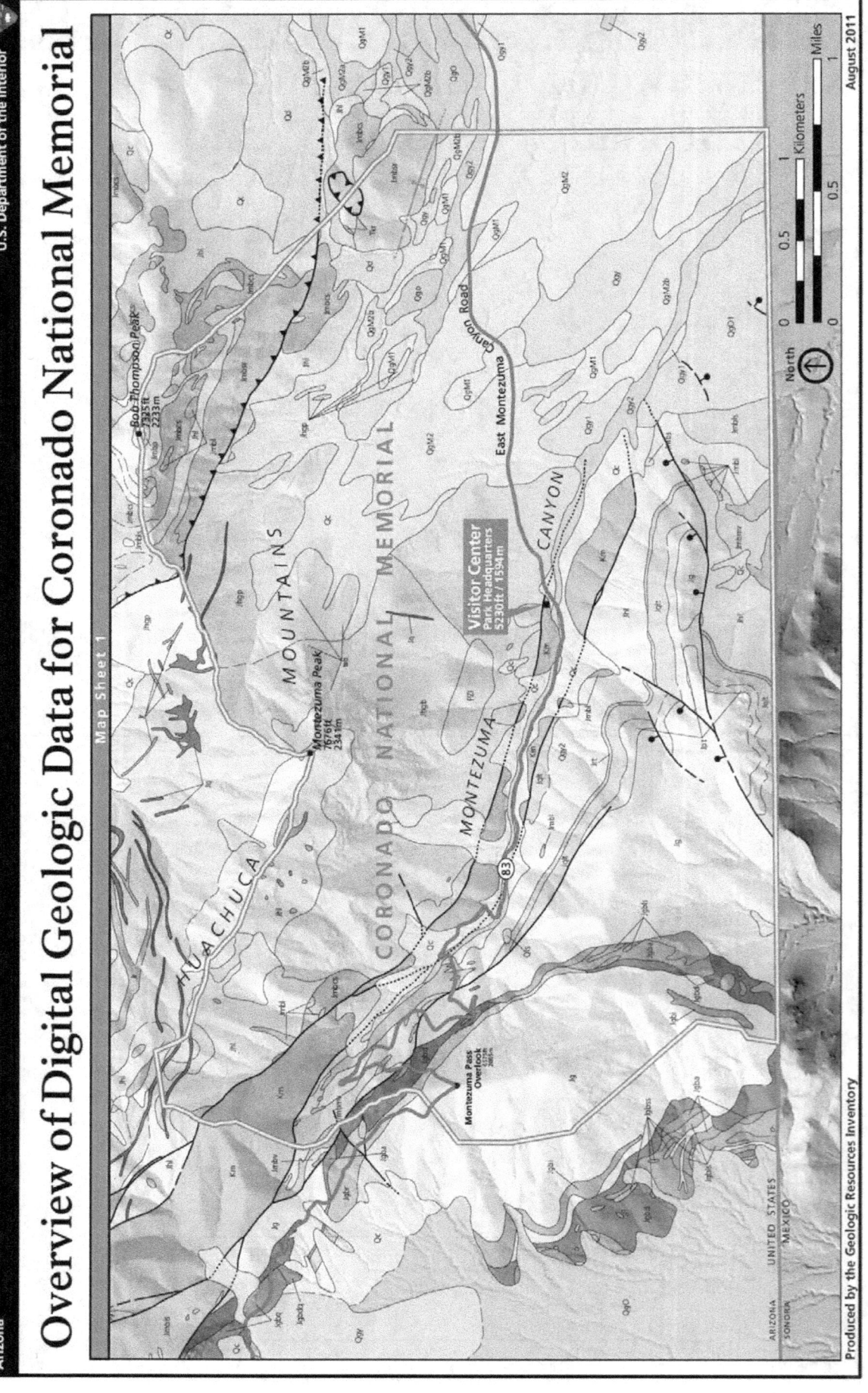

Map Sheet 1

Map Unit Properties Table: Coronado National Memorial

Units that are not mapped within Coronado National Memorial boundaries are colored gray.

Age	Unit Name (Symbol)	Features and Description	Erosion Resistance	Suitability for Infrastructure	Hazards	Paleontological Resources	Cultural Resources	Caves/Karst	Mineral Occurrence	Habitat	Recreation	Geologic Significance
QUATERNARY — Holocene	Colluvium (Qc)	Gravelly sand with abundant cobbles in distributary flow areas of alluvial fans. Deposited at the base of gentle slopes or hillsides.	Sand is less resistant than cobbles.	Roads; Visitor Center.	Potential creep if toe of slope cut.	None documented.	Possible American Indian sites.	None documented.	Sand and gravel.	Gamma grass; lovegrasses.	Hiking in canyon.	Recent deposit.
	Lake deposits (Qls)	Light-olive-brown to orange-brown, commonly fissile shale and siltstone, evaporites, and fine- to very-fine-grained sandstone. Locally gypsiferous.	Low.	Not mapped in the memorial.	None.	Unknown.	Unknown.	None documented.	Gypsum.	Gypsum limits plant growth.	Limited exposure in backcountry.	Records seasonal deposition.
	Talus deposits (Qt)	Unconsolidated rock material derived from and lying at the base of very steep rocky slopes, especially the steep cliffs of Cb. Most mapped talus deposits contain scarp areas as well as slope deposits.	High for unconsolidated sediment.	Low.	Rocks may shift. Overhanging cliff collapse.	None documented.	None documented.	None documented.	None documented.	Habitat for small animals.	Not advisable; rocks may shift, safety issue.	Evidence of mass wasting.
	Debris flow deposits (Qdf)	Unsorted to poorly sorted, unstratified to poorly stratified, clay- to boulder-sized matrix-supported deposits formed by sediment-dominated flow. May include nearly intact slumped blocks of bedrock several meters long.	Variable. Clay and silt less resistant than coarser material.	Low. Not advisable to build in debris-flow paths.	Damage to infrastructure if in debris-flow paths.	None documented.	None documented.	None documented.	None documented.	Sparse vegetation on recent debris-flow deposits.	Past debris flows damaged picnic areas and other infrastructure.	Major process in channel modification.
	Debris fans (Qdp)	Fan-shaped or planar surfaces that are active only during intense periods of precipitation. Mapped on lower canyon slopes well north of the memorial.	Variable grain size and surface cement.	Not mapped in the memorial.	None. Forms gentle slopes.	Unknown.	Possible American Indian sites.	None documented.	Landscape feature (not a lithic unit).	Lower valley vegetation.	Picnic area and secondary road.	Intense precipitation events.
	Alluvium (Qal)	Recent gravels along Holocene stream drainages. Sand, silt, and gravel in narrow washes; material on alluvial fans from season flooding; sometimes and colluvium. Mapped in the southwest corner of the map. Primarily San Pedro River channel and floodplain to the east.	Variable. Silt less resistant than sand and gravel.	Low. Associated with stream channels.	Potential flooding.	Unknown, but limited due to flooding and erosion.	Any sites present possibly destroyed by water erosion.	None documented.	Sand and gravel. May contain placer gold deposits.	Riparian vegetation susceptible to flooding.	Hiking along stream channels.	Regional aquifer.
Holocene	Terrace gravels: Qgy, Qgy2, Qgy1, QgM2b, QgM2, QgM2a-QgM1	Qgy, Qgy2, and Qgy: Terrace, channel, and alluvial-fan deposits of gravel, gravelly sand, sand, and silt with abundant cobbles and boulders. Qgy is a general designation for areas too small to map at this scale. Qgy2: Modern terrace gravels, channel deposits, and gravel bars. Qgy1: Younger terrace and alluvial-fan deposits. Generally finer-grained toward and distal portions of the deposits.	Variable	Provide relatively flat surfaces but limited areal extent.	Flash flooding could erode terrace.	None documented.	Possible American Indian sites.	None documented.	Gravel. Placer gold deposits discovered outside the memorial	Gamma grass; lovegrasses.	Suitable for hiking.	The vertical and lateral channel erosion represents periods of climate fluctuations.
Pleistocene		QgM2b: Stream terraces and abandoned fan remnants. Silt, sand, and extremely gravelly sand; abundant cobbles near mountains and in terraces along larger channels; distal deposits are very fine-grained (clay). QgM2: Areas of broadly defined terrace and abandoned fan deposits.	Variable. Finer-grained sediment less resistant.	High. Contains roads; ranches.	Occasional flooding from intense precipitation.	Pleistocene and Holocene fossils possible.	Possible American Indian sites.	None documented.	Sand and gravel.	Gamma grass, lovegrasses and other low-elevation plants.	Suitable for hiking.	
		QgM2a: Older stream terraces and abandoned fan remnants. Very similar to younger QgM2b deposits (same composition). Distinguished by deeper dissection and greater soil-profile development.	Variable. Finer-grained sediment less resistant.	Minor exposures. Associated with swales and gullies.	Occasional flooding.	Pleistocene and Holocene fossils possible.	Possible American Indian sites.	None documented.	Sand and gravel.	Low-elevation plants.	Suitable for hiking.	
		QgM1: Mostly fan remnants and local stream terraces. Composed of gravelly to extremely gravelly sand and silt. Concentrations of reddened pebbles and cobbles overlie red clay surfaces. Characterized by relatively narrow, curvilinear, discontinuous uplands dissected by intervening swales and gullies. Depth of dissection is commonly 5 to 8 m (16 to 26 ft).	Silt is less resistant than sand and gravel.	Not mapped in the memorial.	Minor flooding with occasional intense storm.	Pleistocene and Holocene fossils possible.	Possible American Indian sites.	None documented.	Sand and gravel.	Gamma grass; lovegrasses and other low-elevation plants.	Suitable for hiking.	

Units that are not mapped within Coronado National Memorial boundaries are colored gray.

Age	Unit Name (Symbol)	Features and Description	Erosion Resistance	Suitability for Infrastructure	Hazards	Paleontological Resources	Cultural Resources	Caves/Karst	Mineral Occurrence	Habitat	Recreation	Geologic Significance
QUATERNARY — Pleistocene	Terrace Gravels: QgQ, QgQ2, QgQ1 — QgQ: Piedmont gravels (undefined). Areas of broadly defined lower and upper piedmont deposits.		Low.	Minor, isolated exposure.	None.	Pleistocene fossils possible.	Possible American Indian sites.	None documented.	Possible placer gold deposits outside the memorial.	Gamma grass; lovegrasses.	Hiking.	Deposited during a time of relative landscape stability. Extensive pediment formation. QgQ2 may be substantially older than 700,000 years in some places
		QgQ2: Gravels of the lower and middle piedmont. Coarse, carbonate-cemented alluvial gravels, generally less than 1 m (3.3 ft) thick, capping basin fill (QTbf) over a widespread erosional surface. Mapped well north of the memorial.	Moderate to high. (carbonate cement in basin center).	Not mapped in the memorial.	None. Forms gentle slopes in the basin.	Pleistocene and Holocene fossils possible.	Possible American Indian sites.	None documented.	Gravel.	Basin interior vegetation.	Limited due to position within the basin.	
		QgQ1: Gravelly sand and silt of the upper and middle piedmont. Generally coarser than younger deposits in those areas. Dark red-stained cobbles overly strongly-reddened surfaces. Relatively narrow, curvilinear ridges, cut by intervening gullies or ravines to depths of 10 to 25 m (33 to 82 ft).	Variable. Silt is less resistant than sand and gravel.	Contains a road, gullies, and ravines.	No major hazards. Infrequent flooding potential.	Pleistocene and Holocene fossils possible.	Possible American Indian sites.	None documented.	Sand and gravel.	Gamma grass; lovegrasses and other low-elevation plants.	Southeast corner of memorial. Potential for hiking.	Reflect a time of relative landscape stability.
	Lower Pleistocene to upper Pliocene clay and fine-grained sandstone (QTbf)	Generally red-colored with local exposures of buried paleosols. If not capped by QgQ2, forms gently rounded, eroded hills, up to about 15 m (49 ft) above active channels. Mapped in the northeast corner of the map.	Eroded into gently rounded hills.	Not mapped in the memorial.	None.	Pleistocene and Holocene fossils possible.	Possible American Indian sites.	None documented.	Possible clay for brick making.	Basin interior vegetation.	Limited due to position in basin.	Paleosols formed during relative landscape stability.
NEOGENE — TERTIARY	Holocene to Oligocene surficial deposits (QTg)	Gravel, sand, and silt. Mainly basin alluvium. Includes some colluvium and landslide deposits. Light-pinkish-gray, weakly indurated, and with poorly rounded clasts. Mapped 10 km (6 mi) east of Montezuma Ranch.	Variable, depending on clast size and surface cement.	Not mapped in the memorial.	Located within the San Pedro floodplain.	Unknown.	Possible prehistoric and early settler sites.	None documented.	Sand and gravel.	Ranching and agricultural influence.	Developed areas (towns, ranches, railroad, roads).	Basin-fill deposits.
PALEOGENE — TERTIARY	Tertiary Quartz rhyolite porphyry (Thr), Diabase (Tkd)	Thr: Small stock and dikes of crystal-rich (30%) rhyolite. Intrudes tuff and megabreccia on the southeast arm slope of Bob Thompson Peak. Contains 5- to 10-mm (0.2- to 0.4-in) phenocrysts of quartz and potassium feldspar and abundant limestone xenoliths. Tkd: Small plug-like bodies and sills of fine-grained plagioclase and pyroxene diabase. Dusky-red to greenish black. Includes small body of diabase that intrudes Jg on the western side of Montezuma Pass.	High, but minor exposures.	Local, limited exposures near Bob Thompson Peak and Montezuma Pass.	None. Limited areal extent.	None documented. Fossils in extrusive igneous rocks are rare.	None documented.	None documented.	Quartz, potassium feldspar.	Mixed forest of oak, Mexican piñon pine, alligator juniper.	Local exposures near Bob Thompson Peak and Montezuma Pass.	Tkr: May be pyroclastic in origin.
	Tertiary Granodiorite (Tgd), Quartz veins (Tqv), Quartz monzonite (Tqm)	Tgd: Granodiorite to microgranodiorite silts and dikes. Very fine-grained, dark-greenish-gray. Tqv (Tertiary?) Irregular veins of white quartz. Tqm: Sill and dike rock, fine-grained orange to pinkish-orange. Mapped along the western edge of the map, west of the memorial.	High, except where fractured.	Not mapped in the memorial.	Tqm: potential rockfall.	None.	Limited areal extent of outcrops.	None documented.	Quartz.	May be open woodland environment.	Areal extent limited to a ridge of Tqm. No trails noted on map.	Record Tertiary intrusive events.
CRETACEOUS — Upper — Bisbee Group	Fort Crittenden Formation (Kfc)	Grayish-yellow and reddish-brown shale, reddish-brown and greenish-gray clay-rich sandstone, and interbedded pebble conglomerate, weathers light brown. More than 460 m (1,500 ft) thick. Mapped in Save Canyon, located on the western edge of map, far from memorial.	Variable depending on local cementation.	Not mapped in the memorial.	None. Forms gentle slopes.	In general, Kfc is not considered to contain fossils.	Possible prehistoric and early settler sites.	None documented.	No significant minerals.	Lower elevation grasses, shrubs, and mesquite trees.	Limited areal extent. No trails noted.	Initial Laramide Orogeny deposits in the area.
CRETACEOUS — Lower — Bisbee Group	Cintura Formation (Kc)	Pale-red mudstone and siltstone, greyish-pink cross-laminated arkosic sandstone, and minor light-olive-gray clay-rich sandstone. Thin beds of clay-rich limestone in lower part. Thickness: 180 to 370 m (600 to 1,200 ft).	Variable. Mudstone low; limestone high.	Not mapped in the memorial.	None. Forms gentle slopes.	Unknown.	Limited areal extent.	None documented.	No significant minerals.	Low-elevation grasses, shrubs, and mesquite.	Mapped in Save Canyon, west of the memorial.	Marine regression.

Units that are not mapped within Coronado National Memorial boundaries are colored gray.

Age	Unit Name (Symbol)	Features and Description	Erosion Resistance	Suitability for Infrastructure	Hazards	Paleontological Resources	Cultural Resources	Caves/Karst	Mineral Occurrence	Habitat	Recreation	Geologic Significance
CRETACEOUS (Lower) — Bisbee Group	Mural Limestone (Kmu)	Medium-gray limestone, greenish-gray calcareous siltstone, and minor reddish-brown mudstone. Limestone dominant in upper part; shale and siltstone dominant in lower part. About 180 m (600 ft) thick.	Variable. Mudstone: low; limestone: high.	Not mapped in the memorial.	None. Limited areal extent.	Unknown. May contain mollusk fossils.	Limited areal extent.	None documented.	No significant minerals.	Low-elevation grasses, shrubs, and mesquite.	Mapped in Save Canyon, west of the memorial.	Maximum marine transgression in the Bisbee basin.
	Morita Formation (Km)	Fine- to medium-grained, well-sorted, quartz sandstone interbedded with red to maroon siltstone and shale. Exposed in a series of complex fault slices in a zone of imbricate reverse faults within Montezuma Canyon. Fractures in shale layers are at high angle to sandstone beds. Rests on coarse volcaniclastic conglomerate of Jlg. Unconformable contacts locally.	High.	Low. Exposures in fault slices on slopes in Montezuma Canyon.	Potential rockfall in Miller Peak area and slumping in canyon.	Oyster-bearing limestone in upper part. Petrified wood outside of memorial.	Possible artifacts from the State of Texas mine. Possible prehistoric sites.	None reported in the southern Huachuca Mountains.	New Hartford and New Reef mineral districts. North of the memorial, pyrite, sphalerite, hematite, galena, chalcopyrite, limonite, scheelite in quartz veins.	Low- to mid-elevation vegetation types (grasses to open woodlands).	Exposed along the Coronado Cave Trail and hiking trails on Miller Peak.	Deposited on a slowly subsiding detrital plain.
JURASSIC — Bisbee Group		Jgsi: Aphyric (without phenocrysts) basaltic andesite sills intruding Jlg. In other areas, similar flows lie between Jlg and the chert-bearing basal conglomerate of Km. Mapped northwest of the memorial.	Less resistant than the main body of Jlg.	Not mapped in the memorial.	Rockfall potential.	None documented. Fossils in extrusive igneous rocks are rare.	Potential cultural sites (prehistoric hunting locations) on steep slopes.	None documented.	No significant minerals.	Steep slopes may limit vegetation.	Backcountry hiking and camping potential.	Emplacement into wet Jlg sediment.
		Jgbi: Aphyric, dark-colored to rusty brown, medium- to fine-grained basaltic andesite sills. Mapped on western and southern slopes of Montezuma Pass and Coronado Peak, southwestern part of memorial.	Less resistant than the main body of Jlg.	Low. Linear outcrop on steep slope.	Rockfall potential.	None documented. Fossils in extrusive igneous rocks are rare.	Minimal exposure on steep slopes.	None documented.	No phenocrysts.	Rocky slopes limit vegetation.	Limited exposure on remote slopes.	Intrudes and is younger than Jlg.
	Glance Conglomerate (Jga, Jgbi, Jlg, Jgby)	Jlg: Main body of Glance Conglomerate. Volcaniclastic conglomerate. Thick unit of cobble- to boulder-sized conglomerate. Clasts range from pebbles to 1- to 2-m (3.3- to 6.6-ft) diameter boulders. Clasts are quartz rhyolite and crystal-poor rhyolite tuffs and fragments of the intervening lithic-rich tuff and arkosic sandstone. Clasts of Paleozoic limestone are generally absent in the lower 50 to 100 m (160 to 330 ft). Gradual upward transition from non-stratified, matrix-supported conglomerate to crudely stratified, poorly sorted, clast-supported conglomerate. Dacite tuff, andesitic-dacitic lava clasts, and increased occurrence of Paleozoic limestone clasts replace the dominant rhyolite clasts. Above the landslide breccia units, the dominant clasts are andesitic to dacite lavas that include an increasing component of porphyritic intrusive rocks.	High.	Steep slopes prohibit excessive development. Roads, trails, and overlook with facilities exist on Jlg.	Potential rockfall and landsliding in ephemeral stream drainages. Abandoned mines along Crest Trail presents a potential visitor-safety hazard	No in-situ flora or fauna. Clasts of Paleozoic Naco Group limestone may contain fossils (Tweet et al. 2008).	Possible prehistoric sites and artifacts from late 19th century to early 20th century mining activity.	No natural caves.	Crest Trail contains shafts, adits, and tailing piles from past mining activity for lead and zinc ores. North of the memorial: galena, scheelite, chalcopyrite, bornite, and ores of gold, silver, and tungsten in quartz veins (New Reef mineral district).	Mid-elevation open oak woodlands to upper-elevation rocky hillsides and mixed forest of oak, Mexican piñon pine, and alligator juniper.	Montezuma Pass overlook; hiking.	Deposition in alluvial-fan systems that rimmed local fault-block mountain ranges.
	Glance Conglomerate	Jgp: Dark-colored, coarsely porphyritic andesite with plagioclase and weathered hornblende phenocrysts in a dark-gray groundmass.	Least resistant unit in Jlg.	Not mapped in the memorial.	Steep slopes; Rockfall potential.	None documented. Fossils in extrusive igneous rocks are rare.	Narrow outcrop; limited access.	None documented.	Hornblende.	Rocky slopes.	Steep slopes; back-country hiking.	Volcanic activity.
	Landslide breccia (Jgbr, Jgu, Jgbdq, Jgba, Jgbd, Jgbu, Jgbls, Jgbss)	Jgbr: Blocks of orange arkosic to arenitic sandstone and lithic-rich, sparse quartz rhyolite tuff. Jgbd: Blocks of crystal-rich dacite tuff. Jgbu: Blocks of pre-Montezuma Caldera andesite and dacite lava. Jgbls: Blocks of Paleozoic limestone.	High.	Low. Narrow unit within Jlg on steep slopes.	Potential rockfall and landsliding in ephemeral stream drainages.	Possible marine invertebrate fossils in Paleozoic limestone blocks.	Possible American Indian hunting structures on steep slopes.	None documented.	Quartz.	Rocky slopes. Mid-elevation vegetation.	Crossed by road to Montezuma Pass and trail to Coronado Peak.	Wedge- and sheet-deposits derived from Montezuma Caldera collapse to the south.
		Blocks of landslide breccia found near the mouth of Copper Canyon, southwestern part of the map. Not mapped in the memorial. Jgu: Quartz-bearing rhyolite porphyry lava found. Jgbdq: Brecciated dacite and quartz-bearing lavas. Jgbu: Quartz and potassium feldspar-bearing rhyolite porphyry. Jgbss: Slightly siliceous, tan quartzose sandstone, probably largely derived from the Permian Scherrer Formation (Ps).	High.	Not mapped in the memorial.	Isolated outcrops of limited distribution. Minor rockfall potential.	None documented. Fossils in extrusive igneous rocks are rare.	Potential historic mining sites. Prospect pits nearby.	None documented.	Quartz, potassium feldspar.	Rocky slopes with south-western aspect.	Localized, limited exposures. Steep slopes.	Nearly instantaneous deposition, as from a large earthquake.

Units that are not mapped within Coronado National Memorial boundaries are colored gray.

Age	Unit Name (Symbol)	Features and Description	Erosion Resistance	Suitability for Infrastructure	Hazards	Paleontological Resources	Cultural Resources	Caves/Karst	Mineral Occurrence	Habitat	Recreation	Geologic Significance
JURASSIC	Jurassic intrusive and volcanic rocks (Jij)	Rhyolite porphyry. Irregular dikes and small stocks of flow-banded rhyolite porphyry containing 10-15% small, 1- to 3-mm (0.04- to 0.1-in) phenocrysts of quartz and potassium feldspar.	High.	Low. Linear features.	Minor exposures in remote northern areas.	None documented. Fossils in extrusive igneous rocks are rare.	Doubtful. Local exposures in northern area.	None documented.	Quartz, potassium feldspar.	Higher elevation vegetation.	Remote area. Minor exposures.	Igneous intrusive dike.
	Jurassic intrusive and volcanic rocks (Jrp, Jqr, Jr, Jd)	Jrp: Rhyolite porphyry. Pale-red, aphanitic, with prominent quartz and feldspar phenocrysts intruded into coarse-grained granite. Jqr: Quartz rhyolite porphyry intrusions. No detailed description. Jr: Irregular dikes of flow-banded dacite porphyry. Contains 10-15% phenocrysts of potassium and plagioclase feldspar. Jd: Dikes. Mainly rhyolitic porphyry dikes and sills. Isolated outcrops located northwest of the memorial.	High.	Not mapped in the memorial	Linear dikes of limited extent pose little hazard.	None documented. Fossils in extrusive igneous rocks are rare.	Potential for cultural sites is low. Outcrops are linear features with limited areal extent.	None documented.	Potassium and plagioclase feldspar; quartz.	Igneous dikes offer limited opportunity for plant growth.	Limited. Most exposures are too small to be mapped at a scale of 1:24,000.	Jurassic intrusions into Jurassic granite.
	Huachuca Granite (Jhgb, Jhgp)	Jhgb: Equigranular granite. Pink to pinkish-gray, medium- to coarse-grained [3 to 6 mm, (0.1 to 0.2 in)]. Contains quartz, potassium and plagioclase feldspar, and lesser biotite. Cut by narrow aplites. Sparse mafic inclusions. Pods [1 to 2 m, (3.3 to 6.6 ft)] of coarse pegmatite mapped near the top of the pluton near Montezuma Peak. Jhgp: Porphyritic granite. Gray to grayish-pink. Phenocrysts [1 to 3 cm, (0.4 to 1.2 in)] of potassium feldspar in a coarse-grained [5 mm, (0.2 in)] matrix of potassium feldspar, plagioclase, quartz, biotite, and amphibole. Contains mafic inclusions, only rarely cut by aplite.	High.	Low. Rugged topography in the memorial's northern part; steep slopes.	Potential rock fall, debris-flow scarps, and landsliding	None.	Possible prehistoric sites and artifacts from past mining activity.	None documented.	Potassium feldspar, galena, pyrite, sphalerite. North of memorial, minor gold-silver ore produced from Paleogene quartz veins.	High elevation vegetation: mixed forest of oak, Mexican piñon pine, and alligator juniper.	Exposed along the Coronado Cave Trail, but primarily exposed in remote, northern part of the memorial.	Intruded into the Naco Group following the collapse of the Montezuma Caldera.
	Huachuca Granite (Jhh, Jhpa, Jhgf, Jhgh, Jhu)	Units of Huachuca Granite. Isolated exposures of limited areal extent. Mapped north of the memorial. Jhh: Dark-greenish-black basalt dikes. 1- to 2-mm (0.04- to 0.08-in) phenocrysts of plagioclase and pyroxene in an aphanitic matrix. Jhpa: Light-tan to pale-gray, fine-grained equigranular aplite. Forms discontinuous dikes and sill-like bodies. Jhgf: Pinkish-gray to buff-colored, fine-grained granite; equal amounts of quartz, potassium and plagioclase feldspar; lesser biotite. Jhgh: Dark- to medium-gray, equigranular amphibole granite. Hornblende, potassium feldspar, plagioclase; lesser quartz, biotite. Jhu: Undifferentiated granitic intrusive.	High.	Not mapped in the memorial	Potential rockfall and landsliding in Jhu, the dominant unit.	None.	Jhu: Possible prehistoric sites and artifacts from past mining activity.	None documented.	Hornblende, potassium feldspar, plagioclase, quartz, biotite, pyroxene. Huachuca granite is in the New Harford and New Reef mineral districts.	High elevation vegetation: mixed forest of oak, Mexican piñon pine, and alligator juniper.	Jhu: Backcountry recreation.	Jhh: Some irregular contacts suggest emplacement into granite that was still cooling.
	Parker Canyon Caldera Quartz rhyolite tuff (Jpt)	Crystal-rich, red-brown rhyolite tuff. Contains 20-30% phenocrysts of quartz and potassium feldspar with minor plagioclase and sparse biotite. Caps the volcanic sequence in this area: 30 to 40 m (100 to 130) ft) thick.	High.	Low. Thin outcrop band on steep slopes. Overlies Jqlt.	Rockfall potential.	None documented. Fossils in extrusive igneous rocks are rare.	None documented. Relatively thin outcrop layer on steep slopes.	None documented.	Quartz, plagioclase, potassium feldspar.	Thin outcrop band. Rocky slopes; sparse vegetation.	Crossed by Joe's Canyon Trail.	Ponded within the Montezuma Caldera
	Sandstone and lithic-rich tuff (Jqlt)	Interbedded orange to red-orange arkosic and quartz sandstones, siltstones, and conglomerate interbedded with pink to pinkish-gray, thin, poorly to moderately welded, lithic-rich ash-flow tuffs. Tuffs contain sparse (less than 10%), 1- to 2-mm (0.04- to 0.08-in) phenocrysts of quartz and potassium feldspar. Tuff layers include thin-bedded [10 to 50 cm, (3.4 to 5.9 in)] ash-fall tuffs.	High. Welded tuff more resistant than sandstone and siltstone.	Low. Thin outcrop band parallels Jqt on steep slopes.	Rockfall potential.	None documented. Fossils in extrusive igneous rocks are rare.	None documented. Relatively thin outcrop layer on steep slopes.	None documented.	Quartz, potassium feldspar.	Thin outcrop band. Rocky slopes; sparse vegetation.	Crossed by Joe's Canyon Trail.	Tuffs may be early eruptive phases from the Parker Canyon Caldera.
	Turkey Canyon Caldera Crystal-poor rhyolite tuff (Jrt)	Grey to red-gray, crystal-poor rhyolite tuff containing about 5-10% phenocrysts of potassium feldspar. Present only in the southern part of the memorial where it directly overlies Jbl.	High.	Low. Thin outcrop band parallels Jqt on steep slopes.	Rockfall potential.	None documented. Fossils in extrusive igneous rocks are rare.	None documented. Relatively thin outcrop layer on steep slopes.	None documented.	Potassium feldspar.	Thin outcrop band. Rocky slopes; sparse vegetation.	Crossed by Joe's Canyon Trail.	Turkey Canyon Caldera volcanic deposit.
	Montezuma Caldera Crystal-rich dacite tuff and associated collapse breccia (Jbl)	Crystal-rich dacite tuff. Red-brown to dark-greenish-gray to dark-green dacite tuff containing about 30% phenocrysts of plagioclase, minor biotite, and sparse quartz. Lithic content varies from less than 5% to 30%. Mapped south of Montezuma Canyon, along the ridge to Montezuma Peak, on Bob Thompson Peak, and east of Miller Peak. Low-grade metamorphism north of Montezuma Canyon.	High.	Low in the northern Montezuma Peak area, more accessible south of Montezuma Canyon.	Debris chutes and rockfall potential in rugged topography north of Montezuma Canyon.	None documented.	Possible prehistoric sites and remnants of past mining activity.	None documented.	Plagioclase, quartz, biotite, epidote.	North: Rocky debris slides and high elevation vegetation. South: Mid-elevation vegetation.	Crossed by the Arizona Crest Trail (northwest) and by Joe's Canyon Trail.	Records synchronous infilling of the collapsing Montezuma Caldera.

Units that are not mapped within Coronado National Memorial boundaries are colored gray.

Age	Unit Name (Symbol)	Features and Description	Erosion Resistance	Suitability for Infrastructure	Hazards	Paleontological Resources	Cultural Resources	Caves/Karst	Mineral Occurrence	Habitat	Recreation	Geologic Significance
JURASSIC	Montezuma Caldera Sandstone and limestone megabreccia (Jbmsl)	Mixed blocks of meter- to several meter-sized well-sorted quartz sandstone and limestone megabreccia of Montezuma Caldera. Mapped in Hunter Canyon, well north of the memorial.	High.	Not mapped in the memorial.	Rockfall on steep slopes.	Possible fossils in limestone megabreccia.	Exposures of limited areal extent.	None documented.	None documented.	Mixed elevation vegetation.	Crossed by unimproved road.	Associated with Jhl.
	Montezuma Caldera Collapse Breccia (Jm bls, Jmbl, Jmbcs, Jmbc, Jmbmv, Jmbv, Jmbar, Jmbsa, Jmbs, Jmbap, Jmbp)	Jmbs: Masses of dark-gray to white limestone blocks up to 1 km (0.6 mi) long near Montezuma Canyon. Thick breccia lenses of mixed limestone and andesite south of Montezuma Canyon; smaller limestone masses completely enclosed by dacite tuff near Montezuma Peak. Limestone is strongly foliated and recrystallized to marble northeast of a major Cochise thrust fault. Jmbl: Small, less than 1 m (3 3 ft) to several-meter-sized individual blocks of undistinguishable limestone.	High.	Suitable on gentle slopes adjacent to international border.	Exposures on steep-slopes may contribute to rockfall or landslides.	Possible marine invertebrate fossils if limestone not recrystallized to marble.	Possible prehistoric sites although exposures are of limited areal extent.	None documented.	Marble.	Variety of elevations from slopes adjacent to alluvial fans to high elevations east of Miller Peak.	Exposures near the Montezuma Canyon Road. Isolated exposures off-trail in other parts of the memorial.	Unit resulted from collapse of the Montezuma Caldera.
		Jmbcs: Blocks of light green to greenish-white, aphanitic hornfels with boulder- to mega-block inclusions of recrystallized limestone. Includes coarse skarn-type calc-silicate rock in contact metamorphosed megabreccia adjacent to Huachuca granite. Jmbc: Fine-grained to aphanitic greenish-white hornfels, strongly foliated, probably metavolcanic in origin.	High.	Low. Steep slopes south of Bob Thompson Peak.	Rockfall and landslide potential	None documented.	Exposures of limited areal extent on steep slopes. None documented.	None documented.	Garnet, vesuvianite, epidote, Pyroxene.	High-elevation vegetation and rocky slopes.	No formal trails. Backcountry hiking.	Probably formed from hot fluids in contact with clayey limestone megabreccia.
		Jmbmv: Red-brown to dark-gray shattered blocks of pre-caldera andesite and dacite lava. Mapped south of Montezuma Canyon, as isolated blocks 10 to 900 m (33 to 1,600 ft) thick enclosed by tuff near Montezuma Peak and Miller Peaks. Most common lava type contains 20-30% angular plagioclase phenocrysts [2 to 3 mm, (0.08 to 0.1 in)] in a red-brown matrix. Fine-grained, red-gray to gray lava collapse breccia on Montezuma Pass. Blocks of gray lava with 5-15% subangular plagioclase phenocrysts [2 to 3 mm, (0.8 to 0.1 in)] are widespread, but less common than other lava types. Jmbc: Individual small, less than 1 m (3 3 ft) to several meter-sized blocks of pre-caldera andesite and dacite lava.	High.	Isolated outcrops of limited areal extent on steep slopes north of Montezuma Canyon or adjacent to international border.	Rockfall potential north of Montezuma Canyon.	None documented.	Limited exposures on steep slopes. None documented.	None documented.	Plagioclase.	High-elevation vegetation and rocky slopes.	Near Arizona Crest Trail in northwestern part of memorial. Remote outcrops.	Abundance of andesitic-dacitic blocks near the southern margin of the caldera suggests that a locus of volcanic centers may have been present in this area prior to caldera collapse.
		Jmbsa: Large blocks of laminated sandstone interbedded with siltstone and red shale, marl, and limestone-clast conglomerate. Tan, finely laminated, well-sorted feldspathic arenite. Red to red-brown siltstones and shales with well-developed fractures and small folds related to later thrusting.	Variable. Sandstone more resistant than siltstone and shale.	Low. Steep slopes near fault south of Bob Thompson Peak.	Rockfall and landslide potential.	None documented.	Possible archeological remains of mobile foragers.	Paleokarst features on blocks of limestone conglomerate.	None documented.	High-elevation vegetation and rocky slopes.	No trails. Backcountry hiking.	Paleokarst deposits formed prior to caldera collapse.
		Jmbs: Smaller blocks and shattered masses of tan, well-sorted, quartz sandstone. Probably originally derived from Ps. Jmbc: Individual, small, less than 1-m (3.3-ft) blocks of tan, well-sorted sandstone similar to Jmbs. Neither unit is mapped in the memorial.	Sandstone weakly cemented, will erode more easily than rest of unit.	Not mapped in the memorial	Unknown. Outcrops too small to map at map scale.	Unknown, but highly unlikely to find fossils in megabreccia.	Limited areal extent.	Unknown.	None documented.	Unknown. Limited areal extent.	Unknown. Limited areal extent.	May have derived from the Scherrer Formation (Ps).
		Jmbap: Blocks of green phyllite and red shale/siltstone intermixed with limestone megabreccia. Jmbp: Individual, 1 cm (3 3 ft) to several meter-sized blocks of red and green shale and phyllite.	The areal extents of these two units are too small to be represented on the 1:24,000 scale of the reference map.									Chaotic blocks of caldera-collapse breccia.
						REGIONAL UNCONFORMITY						
PERMIAN — Cisuralian (lower) — Naco Group	Scherrer Formation (Ps)	Quartzite sandstone and medium-gray dolomite. White to yellowish-gray upper sandstone unit; light-brown lower sandstone unit. Both units are laminated to thinly bedded and locally cross-laminated. Contains medium-gray dolomite beds and red mudstone at base. Quartz and chert nodules common. Mapped as isolated lenses of bedrock on the edge bordering Sawmill Canyon, northwest section of the reference map.	High, but less resistant than surrounding dolomite of Pc.	Not mapped in or near the memorial.	Limited areal extent, but steep slopes may contain unstable talus slopes.	Echinoid spines, bryozoans, brachiopods, crinoids, and burrows.	Possible prehistoric lithic-processing sites.	None documented.	Chert.	High-elevation vegetation, rocky knobs.	Backcountry use in Coronado National Forest.	Marine transgression.

Units that are not mapped within Coronado National Memorial boundaries are colored gray.

Age	Unit Name (Symbol)	Features and Description	Erosion Resistance	Suitability for Infrastructure	Hazards	Paleontological Resources	Cultural Resources	Caves/Karst	Mineral Occurrence	Habitat	Recreation	Geologic Significance
PERMIAN — Cisuralian (Lower); Naco Group	Epitaph Dolomite (Pe)	Upper member: medium- to dark-gray, medium- to thick-bedded resistant dolomite and limestone; local chert and quartz nodules. Middle member: yellowish-gray to pale-pink marl, siltstone, and argillaceous dolomite, local beds of gypsum. Lower member: medium- and dark-gray to brownish gray medium- to thin-bedded dolomite. Total thickness about 260 m (860 ft). Surrounds the knobs of Pc's in Sawmill Canyon.	Variable. Dolomite and limestone more resistant than marl, siltstone, and gypsum.	Not mapped in or near the memorial.	Potential rockfall and landslides.	Gastropods, corals, brachiopods, and echinoids. Less fossiliferous than Ps and Pc.	Limited areal extent but possible prehistoric and early mining sites.	None documented, but dissolution caves possible if the dolomite is fractured.	Chert, gypsum.	Steep rocky slopes; high-elevation vegetation.	Backcountry use in Coronado National Forest.	Cross-beds, ripple marks, and fossils indicate shallow-water, restricted marine environments.
	Colina Limestone (Pc)	Medium- to dark-gray limestone. Up to 53-m (175-ft) thicknesses of Pc dolomite locally mapped with Pc in the Huachuca Mountains; total mapped unit about 320 m (1,050 ft) thick. Forms steep slopes in Sawmill Canyon.	High.	Not mapped in or near the memorial.	Potential rockfall and landslides.	Corals, brachiopods, mollusks, and echinoids.	Possible prehistoric and early mining activity sites.	Dissolution caves possible, especially in fractured limestone.	None documented	Steep rocky slopes; high-elevation vegetation.	Backcountry use in Coronado National Forest.	Deposition on an open marine carbonate shelf.
PERMIAN-PENNSYLVANIAN	Earp Formation (PPNe)	Pale-red calcareous siltstone and mudstone. Minor thin-bedded limestone and marl. Thin, locally prominent, chert-pebble conglomerate about 60 m (200 ft) below the top. May be 120 m (400 ft) thick in Huachuca Mountains.										Cyles of transgressions and regressions.
	Horquilla Limestone (PPNh)	Medium-light-gray limestone with interbedded pale-red calcareous siltstone and silty limestone. May be 180 m (600 ft) thick in Huachuca Mountains.	The areal extents of the Earp Formation and Horquilla Limestone are too small to be represented on the 1:24,000 scale of the reference map.									
	Undifferentiated Naco Group (PZu)	Large blocks of altered limestone and dolomitic limestone surrounded by Huachuca granite. Contact metamorphism formed magnetite, hematite, and Fe-sulfide replacement skarn bodies. Other beds within the blocks have been selectively altered to garnet-epidote-wolastonite-pyroxene skarn or fine-grained calc-silicate hornfels. Limestone mostly recrystallized to marble; strongly foliated. Original chert layers within the limestones have been boudinaged, dismembered, and locally folded. Insufficient information to identify specific formations within Naco Group.	High, but less resistant than granite.	Low. Isolated exposures surrounded by granite; caves; fractures.	Potential cave collapse from rare earthquakes.	Possible algal stromatolites (layered algal colonies) along Coronado Cave Trail; marine invertebrates possible in limestone not recrystallized to marble.	Prehistoric projectile points found in the past. Legends of cave use by Apache Indians. Cave in dire need of restoration.	Coronado Cave and associated speleothems (e.g., stalactites, stalagmites, flowstones, and helictites).	Ore at State of Texas mine was mostly zinc with minor amounts of lead, copper, silver, tungsten, manganese, and gold. Calcite, galena, garnet, sphalerite pyrite, willemite, and chalcopyrite.	Caves provide habitat for diverse community of insects and small animals, including bats.	Coronado Cave and trail.	Naco Group units represent transgression and regression events. Units are in the footwall of a regional thrust fault. Intrusion of Huachuca granite caused mineralization.
					REGIONAL UNCONFORMITY							
MISSISSIPPIAN	Escabrosa Limestone (Me)	Medium- to light-gray thick-bedded crinoidal limestone and minor medium- to dark-gray thin-bedded limestone. Probably more than 150 m (500 ft) thick. Mapped to the north in the hanging walls of regional thrust faults.	Thick beds more resistant than thinner beds.	Not mapped in the memorial.	Rockfall and landslide potential on steep slopes.	Crinoids.	Possible prehistoric and early mining sites.	Cave/karst development possible.	Sphalerite and galena at State of Texas mine.	High-elevation vegetation and rocky slopes.	Backcountry use. Forms summit of Ramsey Peak.	Represent a major marine transgression from the southeast. During the Laramide Orogeny, these units were thrust over younger Mesozoic and Paleozoic units.
DEVONIAN	Martin Limestone (Dm)	Medium- to dark-gray dolomite and sandy dolomite with a few thin beds of sandstone and mudstone. About 98 m (320 ft) thick. Mapped in the hanging walls of regional thrust faults, well north of the memorial.	Siltstone less resistant than sandstone and limestone.	Not mapped in the memorial.	Rockfall and landslide potential on steep slopes.	Small brachiopods and some corals.	Possible prehistoric and early mining activity sites.	Dissolution caves in Devonian limestone are common in the southwest.	New Reef mineral district. Scheelite, galena, pyrite, sphalerite, goethite, hematite, limonite, and malachite occur in quartz veins.	High-elevation vegetation and rocky slopes.	Backcountry use in Coronado National Forest.	
					REGIONAL UNCONFORMITY							

Units that are not mapped within Coronado National Memorial boundaries are colored gray.

Age	Unit Name (Symbol)	Features and Description	Erosion Resistance	Suitability for Infrastructure	Hazards	Paleontological Resources	Cultural Resources	Caves/Karst	Mineral Occurrence	Habitat	Recreation	Geologic Significance
CAMBRIAN	Abrigo Limestone (Ca)	Upper part: medium-gray limestone with numerous thin layers of light-brown-weathering silty limestone. Lower part: yellowish-brown shale with minor silty limestone and dolomite strata. Mapped in the hanging walls of regional thrust faults, well north of the memorial.	Variable. Limestone is more resistant to erosion than silty limestone and shale.	Not mapped in the memorial.	Steep slopes may generate rock fall and landslides.	Trilobites, brachiopods.	Possible prehistoric (hunting) and early mining activity sites.	Dissolution caves possible in the limestone.	New Reef mineral district. Scheelite, galena, ores of tungsten, gold, and silver in veins.	Mixed forest in higher elevations.	Backcountry use in Coronado National Forest.	Represent a major marine transgression from the southeast. During the Laramide Orogeny, these units were thrust over younger Mesozoic and Paleozoic units.
CAMBRIAN	Bolsa Quartzite (Cb)	Resistant yellowish- to reddish-brown-weathering siliceous sandstone. About 145 m (475 ft) thick. Mapped in the hanging walls of regional thrust faults, well north of the memorial.	Moderately high.	Not mapped in the memorial.	Potential rock fall and landslides from steep slopes.	Metamorphism of sandstone to quartzite destroyed any fossils.	Possible prehistoric (hunting) and early mining activity sites.	Unknown.	None documented in the southern Huachuca Mountains.	Forest of oak, Mexican piñon pine and alligator juniper.	Backcountry use in Coronado National Forest.	

REGIONAL UNCONFORMITY

Age	Unit Name (Symbol)	Features and Description	Erosion Resistance	Suitability for Infrastructure	Hazards	Paleontological Resources	Cultural Resources	Caves/Karst	Mineral Occurrence	Habitat	Recreation	Geologic Significance
MESOPROTEROZOIC EON	Fine-grained alaskite (Yga)	Fine-grained alkali feldspar granite (alaskite). Composed of quartz and feldspar crystals (holocrystalline). No glassy part. Occurs in a fault sliver. Sheared, metamorphosed, and may be related to Yg.	High.	Not mapped in the memorial.	Minor exposures along faults.	None.	Limited areal extent.	Unlikely due to limited areal extent.	New Reef mineral district. Scheelite, galena, pyrite, earthy hematite, calcite, ores of tungsten and minor gold in quartz veins.	Vegetation may mark fault trace on the surface.	Limited areal extent.	Precambrian igneous intrusions indicate deformation about 1.4 billion years ago.
MESOPROTEROZOIC EON	Porphyritic granite (Yg)	Yellowish- to pinkish-gray coarse-grained porphyritic granite; includes some unmapped areas of fine-grained alaskite. Main map unit north of Miller Canyon. Mapped in the hanging walls of regional thrust faults.	High.	Not mapped in the memorial.	Rock fall and land-slide potential.	None.	Possible prehistoric and early mining activity sites.	Unknown.		Open oak woodlands and mixed forests.	Secondary roads, trails, and other backcountry use in national forest.	

Age	Unit Name (Symbol)	Features and Description	Erosion Resistance	Suitability for Infrastructure	Hazards	Paleontological Resources	Cultural Resources	Caves/Karst	Mineral Occurrence	Habitat	Recreation	Geologic Significance
PALEOZOIC ERA	Sedimentary rocks, undifferentiated (PZu)	Rain Valley (Lower Permian) to Bolsa Quartzite (Middle Cambrian), undifferentiated sedimentary rock.	Variable.	Not mapped in the memorial.	Minor exposures along faults.	None documented.	Unknown.	Unknown.	Unknown.	Unknown.	Limited areal extent.	Only found in fault slices through Yg.

Age	Unit Name (Symbol)	Features and Description	Erosion Resistance	Suitability for Infrastructure	Hazards	Paleontological Resources	Cultural Resources	Caves/Karst	Mineral Occurrence	Habitat	Recreation	Geologic Significance
AGE UNCERTAIN	thin seams of basalt (tkb)	Thin seams of basalt. No further description given in Hon et al. (2007).	Moderately high	Linear features of limited areal extent.	Potential for rock fall on steep slopes.	None.	Unknown	Linear features of limited areal extent.	Unknown.	Linear features of limited areal extent.	Linear features of limited areal extent.	Primarily found in rocks of Jurassic (Huachuca Granite and Montezuma Caldera) and Meso-proterozoic (porphyritic granite) age.

Reference map: Hon, K.A., F. Gray, K.S. Bolm, K.A. Dempsey, and P.A. Pearthree. 2007. A digital geologic map of the Miller Peak, Nicksville, Bob Thompson Peak, and Montezuma Pass Quadrangles, Arizona. U.S. Geological Survey Scientific Investigations Map, SIM unpublished (scale 1:24,000).

Glossary

This glossary contains brief definitions of technical geologic terms used in this report. Not all geologic terms used are referenced. For more detailed definitions or to find terms not listed here please visit: http://geomaps.wr.usgs.gov/parks/misc/glossarya.html. Definitions are based on those in the American Geological Institute Glossary of Geology (fifth edition; 2005).

absolute age. The geologic age of a fossil, rock, feature, or event in years; commonly refers to radiometrically determined ages.

abyssal plain. A flat region of the deep ocean floor, usually at the base of the continental rise.

active margin. A tectonically active margin where lithospheric plates come together (convergent boundary), pull apart (divergent boundary) or slide past one another (transform boundary). Typically associated with earthquakes and, in the case of convergent and divergent boundaries, volcanism. Compare to "passive margin."

alaskite. A type of granite with high percentage of sodium- or potassium-rich feldspar minerals and a low percentage of mafic minerals.

alluvial fan. A fan-shaped deposit of sediment that accumulates where a hydraulically confined stream flows to a hydraulically unconfined area. Commonly out of a mountainous area into an area such as a valley or plain.

alluvium. Stream-deposited sediment.

anticline. A convex-upward ("A" shaped) fold. Older rocks are found in the center.

aphanitic. Describes the texture of fine-grained igneous rocks where the different components are not distinguishable with the unaided eye.

aphyric. Describes the texture of fine-grained or aphanitic igneous rocks that lack coarse (large) crystals.

aplite. A light-colored intrusive igneous rock characterized by a fine-grained texture. Emplaced at a relatively shallow depth beneath Earth's surface.

aquifer. A rock or sedimentary unit that is sufficiently porous that it has a capacity to hold water, sufficiently permeable to allow water to move through it, and currently saturated to some level.

arenite. A general term for sedimentary rocks composed of sand-sized fragments with a pure or nearly pure chemical cement and little or no matrix material between the fragments.

argillaceous. Describes a sedimentary rock composed of a substantial amount of clay.

arkose. A sandstone with abundant feldspar minerals, commonly coarse-grained and pink or reddish.

ash (volcanic). Fine material ejected from a volcano (also see "tuff").

asthenosphere. Earth's relatively weak layer or shell below the rigid lithosphere.

bajada. Geomorphic feature formed from the coalescence of alluvial fans along a basin margin.

basalt. A dark-colored, often low-viscosity, extrusive igneous rock.

basement. The undifferentiated rocks, commonly igneous and metamorphic, that underlie rocks exposed at the surface.

basin (sedimentary). Any depression, from continental to local scales, into which sediments are deposited.

basin (structural). A doubly plunging syncline in which rocks dip inward from all sides.

batholith. A massive, discordant pluton, larger than 100 km^2 (40 mi^2), and often formed from multiple intrusions of magma.

bed. The smallest sedimentary strata unit, commonly ranging in thickness from one centimeter to a meter or two and distinguishable from beds above and below.

bedding. Depositional layering or stratification of sediments.

bedrock. A general term for the rock that underlies soil or other unconsolidated, surficial material.

block (fault). A crustal unit bounded by faults, either completely or in part.

boudinage. A structure common in strongly deformed sedimentary and metamorphic rocks, in which an originally-continuous layer or bed has been stretched, thinned, and broken at regular intervals into bodies resembling "boudins" (sausages).

braided stream. A sediment-clogged stream that forms multiple channels which divide and rejoin.

breccia. A coarse-grained, generally unsorted sedimentary rock consisting of cemented angular clasts greater than 2 mm (0.08 in).

calcareous. Describes rock or sediment that contains the mineral calcium carbonate ($CaCO_3$).

calcite. A common rock-forming mineral: $CaCO_3$ (calcium carbonate).

calc-silicate rock. A metamorphic rock consisting mainly of calcium-bearing silicates and formed by metamorphism of impure limestone or dolomite.

caldera. A large bowl- or cone-shaped depression at the summit of a volcano. Formed by explosion or collapse.

caliche. Hard, calcium-carbonate cemented layer commonly found on or near the surface of arid and semiarid regions.

carbonaceous. Describes a rock or sediment with considerable carbon content, especially organics, hydrocarbons, or coal.

carbonate. A mineral that has CO_3^{-2} as its essential component (e.g., calcite and aragonite).

carbonate rock. A rock consisting chiefly of carbonate minerals (e.g., limestone, dolomite, or carbonatite).

chemical sediment. A sediment precipitated directly from solution (also called nonclastic).

chemical weathering. Chemical breakdown of minerals at Earth's surface via reaction with water, air, or dissolved substances; commonly results in a change in chemical composition more stable in the current environment.

clast. An individual grain or rock fragment in a sedimentary rock, produced by the physical disintegration of a larger rock mass.

clastic. Describes rock or sediment made of fragments of pre-existing rocks (clasts).

clay. Can be used to refer to clay minerals or as a sedimentary fragment size classification (less than 1/256 mm [0.00015 in]).

claystone. Lithified clay having the texture and composition

colluvium. A general term for any loose, heterogeneous, and incoherent mass of soil material and/or rock fragments deposited through the action of surface runoff (rainwash, sheetwash) or slow continuous downslope creep.

concordant. Strata with contacts parallel to the orientation of adjacent strata.

conglomerate. A coarse-grained, generally unsorted, sedimentary rock consisting of cemented, rounded clasts larger than 2 mm (0.08 in).

continental crust. Crustal rocks rich in silica and alumina that underlie the continents; ranging in thickness from 35 km (22 mi) to 60 km (37 mi) under mountain ranges.

continental rise. Gently sloping region from the foot of the continental slope to the deep ocean abyssal plain; it generally has smooth topography but may have submarine canyons.

continental shelf. The shallowly submerged part of a continental margin extending from the shoreline to the continental slope with water depths less than 200 m (660 ft).

continental shield. A continental block of Earth's crust that has remained relatively stable over a long period of time and has undergone minor warping compared to the intense deformation of bordering crust.

continental slope. The relatively steep slope from the outer edge of the continental shelf down to the more gently sloping ocean depths of the continental rise or abyssal plain.

convergent boundary. A plate boundary where two tectonic plates are colliding.

cordillera. A Spanish term for an extensive mountain range; used in North America to refer to all of the western mountain ranges of the continent.

core. The central part of Earth, beginning at a depth of about 2,900 km (1,800 mi), probably consisting of iron-nickel alloy.

country rock. The rock surrounding an igneous intrusion or pluton. Also, the rock enclosing or traversed by a mineral deposit.

craton. The relatively old and geologically stable interior of a continent (also see "continental shield").

crinoid. A marine invertebrate (echinoderm) that uses a stalk to attach itself to a substrate. "Arms" are used to capture food. Rare today, they were very common in the Paleozoic. Crinoids are also called "sea lilies."

cross-bedding. Uniform to highly varied sets of inclined sedimentary beds deposited by wind or water that indicate flow conditions such as water flow direction and depth.

crust. Earth's outermost compositional shell, 10 to 40 km (6 to 25 mi) thick, consisting predominantly of relatively low-density silicate minerals (also see "oceanic crust" and "continental crust").

crystalline. Describes a regular, orderly, repeating geometric structural arrangement of atoms.

debris flow. A moving mass of rock fragments, soil, and mud, in which more than half of the particles of which are larger than sand size.

deformation. A general term for the processes of faulting, folding, and shearing of rocks as a result of various Earth forces such as compression (pushing together) and extension (pulling apart).

delta. A sediment wedge deposited where a stream flows into a lake or sea.

dike. A narrow igneous intrusion that cuts across bedding planes or other geologic structures.

dip. The angle between a bed or other geologic surface and horizontal.

discordant. Describes contacts between strata that cut across or are set at an angle to the orientation of adjacent rocks.

divergent boundary. An active boundary where tectonic plates are moving apart (e.g., a spreading ridge or continental rift zone).

drainage basin. The total area from which a stream system receives or drains precipitation runoff.

ductile. Describes a rock that is able to sustain deformation (folding, bending, or shearing) before fracturing.

dune. A low mound or ridge of sediment, usually sand, deposited by wind. Common dune types include "barchan," "longitudinal," "parabolic," and "transverse" (see respective listings).

eolian. Describes materials formed, eroded, or deposited by or related to the action of the wind. Also spelled "Aeolian."

ephemeral stream. A stream that flows briefly only in direct response to precipitation in the immediate locality and whose channel is at all times above the water table.

evaporite. A sedimentary rock composed primarily of minerals produced from a saline solution as a result of extensive or total evaporation of the solvent (usually water).

extrusive. Describes molten (igneous) material that has erupted onto Earth's surface.

fault. A break in rock along which relative movement has occurred between the two sides.

feldspar. A group of abundant (more than 60% of Earth's crust), light-colored to translucent silicate minerals found in all types of rocks. Usually white and gray to pink. May contain potassium, sodium, calcium, barium, rubidium, and strontium along with aluminum, silica, and oxygen.

feldspathic. Describes a rock containing feldspar.

floodplain. The surface or strip of relatively smooth land adjacent to a river channel and formed by the river. Covered with water when the river overflows its banks.

flowstone. Coatings of calcium carbonate (limestone) that cover many cave surfaces.

fold. A curve or bend of an originally flat or planar structure such as rock strata, bedding planes, or foliation that is usually a product of deformation.

footwall. The mass of rock beneath a fault surface (also see "hanging wall").

formation. Fundamental rock-stratigraphic unit that is mappable, lithologically distinct from adjoining strata, and has definable upper and lower contacts.

fracture. Irregular breakage of a mineral. Any break in a rock (e.g., crack, joint, fault).

granite. An intrusive igneous (plutonic) rock composed primarily of quartz and feldspar. Mica and amphibole minerals are also common. Intrusive equivalent of rhyolite.

graben. A down-dropped structural block bounded by steeply dipping, normal faults (also see "horst").

groundmass. The material between the large crystals in a porphyritic igneous rock. Can also refer to the matrix of a sedimentary rock.

hanging wall. The mass of rock above a fault surface (also see "footwall").

helictites. Delicate speleothems that grow in all directions.

holocrystalline. An igneous rock with a texture composed entirely of crystals.

hornfels. A fine-grained rock composed of a mosaic of grains that are the same size in each dimension without preferred orientation. Typically formed by contact metamorphism, which occurs near the contact with an intrusion of molten material.

horst. Areas of relative "up" between grabens, representing the geologic surface left behind as grabens drop. The best example is the Basin and Range province of Nevada. The basins are grabens and the ranges are weathered horsts. Grabens become a locus for sedimentary deposition (also see "graben").

igneous. Refers to a rock or mineral that originated from molten material; one of the three main classes of rocks—igneous, metamorphic, and sedimentary.

ignimbrite. A pyroclastic flow deposit.

intrusion. A body of igneous rock that invades (pushes into) older rock. The invading rock may be a plastic solid or magma.

island arc. A line or arc of volcanic islands formed over and parallel to a subduction zone.

joint. A break in rock without relative movement of rocks on either side of the fracture surface.

karst topography. Topography characterized by abundant sinkholes and caverns formed by the dissolution of calcareous rocks.

lacustrine. Pertaining to, produced by, or inhabiting a lake or lakes.

lamination. Very thin, parallel layers.

landslide. Any process or landform resulting from rapid, gravity-driven mass movement.

lava. Still-molten or solidified magma that has been extruded onto Earth's surface though a volcano or fissure.

limestone. A sedimentary rock consisting chiefly of calcium carbonate, primarily in the form of the mineral calcite.

lithology. The physical description or classification of a rock or rock unit based on characters such as its color, mineral composition, and grain size.

lithosphere. The relatively rigid outmost shell of Earth's structure, 50 to 100 km (31 to 62 miles) thick, that encompasses the crust and uppermost mantle.

mafic. Describes dark-colored rock, magma, or minerals rich in magnesium and iron. Compare to "felsic."

magma. Molten rock beneath Earth's surface capable of intrusion and extrusion.

mantle. The zone of Earth's interior between the crust and core.

mass wasting. A general term for the downslope movement of soil and rock material under the direct influence of gravity.

matrix. The fine grained material between coarse (larger) grains in igneous rocks or poorly sorted clastic sediments or rocks. Also refers to rock or sediment in which a fossil is embedded.

mechanical weathering. The physical breakup of rocks without change in composition. Synonymous with "physical weathering."

meander. Sinuous lateral curve or bend in a stream channel. An entrenched meander is incised, or carved downward into the surface of the valley in which a meander originally formed. The meander preserves its original pattern with little modification.

member. A lithostratigraphic unit with definable contacts; a member subdivides a formation.

meta–. A prefix used with the name of a sedimentary or igneous rock, indicating that the rock has been metamorphosed.

metamorphic. Describes the process of metamorphism or its results. One of the three main classes of rocks—igneous, metamorphic, and sedimentary.

metamorphism. Literally, a change in form. Metamorphism occurs in rocks through mineral alteration, formation, and/or recrystallization from increased heat and/or pressure.

mineral. A naturally occurring, inorganic crystalline solid with a definite chemical composition or compositional range.

normal fault. A dip-slip fault in which the hanging wall moves down relative to the footwall.

oceanic crust. Earth's crust formed at spreading ridges that underlies the ocean basins. Oceanic crust is 6 to 7 km (3 to 4 miles) thick and generally of basaltic composition.

orogeny. A mountain-building event.

outcrop. Any part of a rock mass or formation that is exposed or "crops out" at Earth's surface.

paleogeography. The study, description, and reconstruction of the physical landscape from past geologic periods.

paleosol. A ancient soil layer preserved in the geologic record.

Pangaea. A theoretical, single supercontinent that existed during the Permian and Triassic periods.

parent material. The unconsolidated organic and mineral material in which soil forms.

passive margin. A margin where no plate-scale tectonism is taking place; plates are not converging, diverging, or sliding past one another. An example is the east coast of North America (compare to "active margin").

pediment. A gently sloping, erosional bedrock surface at the foot of mountains or plateau escarpments.

phenocryst. A coarse (large) crystal in a porphyritic igneous rock.

phyllite. A metamorphosed rock, intermediate in grade between slate and mica schist, with minute crystals of graphite, sericite, or chlorite that impart a silky sheen to the surfaces ("schistosity").

plagioclase. An important rock-forming group of feldspar minerals.

plastic. Describes a material capable of being deformed permanently without rupture.

plate tectonics. The concept that the lithosphere is broken up into a series of rigid plates that move over Earth's surface above a more fluid asthenosphere.

pluton (plutonic). A body of intrusive igneous rock that crystallized at some depth beneath Earth's surface.

porphyry. An igneous rock consisting of abundant coarse crystals in a fine-grained matrix.

porphyritic. Describes an igneous rock wherein the rock contains conspicuously large crystals in a fine-grained groundmass.

potassium feldspar. A feldspar mineral rich in potassium (e.g., orthoclase, microcline, sanidine, adularia).

pyroclastic. Describes clastic rock material formed by volcanic explosion or aerial expulsion from a volcanic vent; also pertaining to rock texture of explosive origin. In the plural, the term is used as a noun.

radiometric age. An age expressed in years and calculated from the quantitative determination of radioactive elements and their decay products.

regression. A long-term seaward retreat of the shoreline or relative fall of sea level.

relative dating. Determining the chronological placement of rocks, events, or fossils with respect to the geologic time scale and without reference to their numerical age.

reverse fault. A contractional high-angle (greater than $45°$) dip-slip fault in which the hanging wall moves up relative to the footwall (also see "thrust fault").

rhyolite. A group of extrusive volcanic rocks, typically porphyritic and commonly exhibiting flow texture, with phenocrysts of quartz and alkali feldspar in a glassy to cryptocrystalline groundmass. The fine-grained extrusive equivalent of granite.

rift. A region of crust where extension results in formation of many related normal faults, often associated with volcanic activity.

rift valley. A depression formed by grabens along the crest of an oceanic spreading ridge or in a continental rift zone.

rock. A solid, cohesive aggregate of one or more minerals.

sand. A clastic particle smaller than a granule and larger than a silt grain, having a diameter in the range of 1/16 mm (0.0025 in) to 2 mm (0.08 in).

sandstone. Clastic sedimentary rock of predominantly sand-sized grains.

scarp. A steep cliff or topographic step resulting from displacement on a fault, or by mass movement, or erosion. Also called an "escarpment."

seafloor spreading. The process by which tectonic plates pull apart and new lithosphere is created at oceanic ridges.

sediment. An eroded and deposited, unconsolidated accumulation of rock and mineral fragments.

sedimentary rock. A consolidated and lithified rock consisting of clastic and/or chemical sediment(s). One of the three main classes of rocks—igneous, metamorphic, and sedimentary.

shale. A clastic sedimentary rock made of clay-sized particles that exhibit parallel splitting properties.

sierra. An often-used Spanish term for a rugged mountain range.

silicate. A compound whose crystal structure contains the SiO_4 tetrahedra.

sill. An igneous intrusion that is of the same orientation as the surrounding rock.

silt. Clastic sedimentary material intermediate in size between fine-grained sand and coarse clay (1/256 to 1/16 mm [0.00015 to 0.002 in]).

siltstone. A variably lithified sedimentary rock composed of silt-sized grains.

skarn. Calcium-bearing silicates derived from nearly pure limestone and dolomite with the introduction of large amounts of silica, aluminum, iron, and magnesium.

slope. The inclined surface of any geomorphic feature or measurement thereof. Synonymous with "gradient."

slump. A generally large, coherent mass movement with a concave-up failure surface and subsequent backward rotation relative to the slope.

speleothem. Any secondary mineral deposit that forms in a cave.

sphene. A usually yellow or brown mineral occurring as an accessory mineral in granitic rocks and in calcium-rich metamorphic rocks. Also called "titanite."

spreading center. A divergent boundary where two lithospheric plates are spreading apart. It is a source of new crustal material.

spring. A site where water issues from the surface due to the intersection of the water table with the ground surface.

stalactites. Calcite deposits that form as water drips from the roof of a cave.

stalagmites. Mounds of calcite that commonly form beneath stalactites from dripping water in a cave.

stock. An igneous intrusion exposed at the surface; less than 100 km^2 (40 mi^2) in size. Compare to "pluton."

strata. Tabular or sheet-like masses or distinct layers of rock.

stratigraphy. The geologic study of the origin, occurrence, distribution, classification, correlation, and age of rock layers, especially sedimentary rocks.

stream. Any body of water moving under gravity flow in a clearly confined channel.

stream channel. A long, narrow depression shaped by the concentrated flow of a stream and covered continuously or periodically by water.

stream terrace. Step-like benches surrounding the present floodplain of a stream due to dissection of previous flood plain(s), stream bed(s), and/or valley floor(s).

strike. The compass direction of the line of intersection of an inclined surface with a horizontal plane.

strike-slip fault. A fault with measurable offset where the relative movement is parallel to the strike of the fault. Said to be "sinistral" (left-lateral) if relative motion of the block opposite the observer appears to be to the left. "Dextral" (right-lateral) describes relative motion to the right.

structure. The attitude and relative positions of the rock masses of an area resulting from such processes as faulting, folding, and igneous intrusions.

subduction zone. A convergent plate boundary where oceanic lithosphere descends beneath a continental or oceanic plate and is carried down into the mantle.

subsidence. The gradual sinking or depression of part of Earth's surface.

suture. The linear zone where two continental landmasses become joined.

syncline. A downward curving (concave-up) fold with layers that dip inward; the core of the syncline contains the stratigraphically-younger rocks.

tectonic. Relating to large-scale movement and deformation of Earth's crust.

terrace. A relatively level bench or step-like surface breaking the continuity of a slope (also see "stream terrace").

terrane. A large region or group of rocks with similar geology, age, or structural style.

terrestrial. Relating to land, Earth, or its inhabitants.

terrigenous. Derived from the land or a continent.

theory. A hypothesis that has been rigorously tested against further observations or experiments to become a generally accepted tenet of science.

thrust fault. A contractional dip-slip fault with a shallowly dipping fault surface (less than 45°) where the hanging wall moves up and over relative to the footwall.

topography. The general morphology of Earth's surface, including relief and locations of natural and anthropogenic features.

trace (fault). The exposed intersection of a fault with Earth's surface.

transgression. Landward migration of the sea as a result of a relative rise in sea level.

trend. The direction or azimuth of elongation of a linear geologic feature.

tuff. Generally fine-grained, igneous rock formed of consolidated volcanic ash.

unconformity. An erosional or non-depositional surface bounded on one or both sides by sedimentary strata. An unconformity marks a period of missing time.

uplift. A structurally high area in the crust, produced by movement that raises the rocks.

volcanic. Describes anything related to volcanoes. Can refer to igneous rock crystallized at or near Earth's surface (e.g., lava).

volcaniclastic. Describes clastic volcanic materials formed by any process of fragmentation, dispersed by any kind of transporting agent, deposited in any environment.

weathering. The physical, chemical, and biological processes by which rock is broken down.

xenolith. A rock particle, formed elsewhere, entrained in magma as an inclusion.

Literature Cited

This section lists references cited in this report. A more complete geologic bibliography is available from the National Park Service Geologic Resources Division.

Anderson, J.L. 1988. Core complexes of the Mojave-Sonoran Desert: Conditions of plutonism, mylonitization, and decompression. Pages 502-525 *in* W.G. Ernst, editor. Metamorphism and crustal evolution of the western United States. Prentice Hall, Englewood Cliffs, New Jersey, USA.

Anderson, T.H., and J.A. Nourse. 2005. Pull-apart basins at releasing bends of the sinistral Late Jurassic Mojave-Sonora fault system. Special Paper – 393. Geological Society of America, Boulder, Colorado, USA.

Anderson, T.H., and L.T. Silver. 2005. The Mojave-Sonora megashear; field and analytical studies leading to the conception and evolution of the hypothesis. Special Paper – 393. Geological Society of America, Boulder, Colorado, USA.

Arizona Department of Water Resources. 2009. Upper San Pedro Basin. Section 3.13 *in* Southeastern Arizona Planning Area. Arizona Water Atlas. Volume 3. Arizona Department of Water Resources, Phoenix, Arizona, USA. (http://www.azwater.gov/AzDWR/StatewidePlanning/WaterAtlas/SEArizona/default.htm). Accessed January 15, 2010.

Arizona Earthquake Information Center. 2010. AEIC Earthquake and Fault Maps. Webpage. Arizona Earthquake Information Center, Northern Arizona University, Flagstaff, Arizona, USA. http://www4.nau.edu/geology/aeic/eq_fault_maps.html (accessed February 2, 2010).

Biek, R.F., G.C. Willis, M.D. Hylland, and H.H. Doelling. 2000. Geology of Zion National Park, Utah. Pages 107-138 *in* D.A. Sprinkel, T.C. Chidsey, Jr., and P.B. Anderson, editors. Geology of Utah's parks and monuments. Publication 28. Utah Geological Association, Salt Lake City, Utah, USA.

Bilodeau, W.L. 1982. Tectonic models for early Cretaceous rifting in southeastern Arizona. Geology 10: 466-470.

Bilodeau, W.L., C.F. Kluth, and L.K. Vedder. 1987. Regional stratigraphic, sedimentologic and tectonic relationships of the Glance Conglomerate in southeastern Arizona. Pages 229-256 *in* W.R. Dickinson and M.A. Klute, editors. Mesozoic rocks of southern Arizona and adjacent areas. Digest 18. Arizona Geological Society, Tucson, Arizona, USA.

Blakey, R.C. 1980. Pennsylvanian and Early Permian paleogeography, southern Colorado Plateau and vicinity. Pages 239-258 *in* T.D. Fouch and E.R. Magathan, editors. Paleozoic paleogeography of west-central United States. Rocky Mountain Section, Society of Economic Paleontologists and Mineralogists, Denver, Colorado, USA.

Blakey, R.C. and R. Knepp. 1989. Pennsylvanian and Permian geology of Arizona. Pages 313-347 *in* J.P. Jenny and S.J. Reynolds, editors. Geologic evolution of Arizona. Digest 17. Arizona Geological Society, Tucson, Arizona, USA.

Brown, J.G. 2005. Water-quality data for selected National Park units, southern and central Arizona and west-central New Mexico, water years 2003 and 2004. Open-File Report 2005-1291. U.S. Geological Survey, Reston, Virginia, USA.

Carlsbad Caverns National Park. 2006. Cave and Karst Management Plan Environmental Assessment. (http://www.nps.gov/cave/parkmgmt/upload/cave_karst_ea_2006.pdf). Accessed May 31, 2010.

Christiansen, E. II, B.J. Kowallis, and M.D. Barton. 1994. Temporal and spatial distribution of volcanic ash in Mesozoic sedimentary rocks of the Western Interior: An alternative record of Mesozoic magmatism. Pages 73-94 *in* M.V. Caputo, J.A. Peterson, and K.J. Franczyk, editors. Mesozoic systems of the Rocky Mountain region, USA. Rocky Mountain Section, Society for Sedimentary Geology, Denver, Colorado, USA.

Coney, P.J. 1979. Tertiary evolution of Cordilleran metamorphic core complexes. Pages 14-28 *in* J.M. Armentrout, M.R. Cole, and H. Terbest, Jr., editors. Cenozoic paleogeography of the western United States. Pacific Section, Society of Economic Paleontologists and Mineralogists, Los Angeles, California, USA.

Conway, C.M. and L.T. Silver. 1989. Early Proterozoic rocks (1710 – 1615 Ma) in central to southeastern Arizona. Pages 165-186 *in* P. Jenny and S.J. Reynolds, editors. Geologic evolution of Arizona. Digest 17. Arizona Geological Society, Tucson, Arizona, USA.

Cook, J.F., A. Youberg, P.A. Pearthree, J.A. Onken, B.J. MacFarlane, D.E. Haddad, E.R. Bigio, and A.L. Kowler. 2009. Mapping of Holocene river alluvium along the San Pedro River, Aravaipa Creek, and Babocomari River, southeastern Arizona. Arizona Geological Survey Digital Map DM-RM-1. (http://repository.azgs.az.gov/uri_gin/azgs/dlio/799). Accessed 8 March 2011.

Davis, G.H. 1987. Saguaro National Monument, Arizona: Outstanding display of the structural characteristics of metamorphic core complexes. Pages 35-40 in M.L. Hill, editor. Centennial Field Guide 1. Cordilleran Section, Geological Society of America, Boulder, Colorado, USA.

Dickinson, W.R. 1979. Cenozoic plate tectonic setting of the Cordilleran region in the United States. Pages 1-13 in J.M. Armentrout, M.R. Cole, and H. Terbest, Jr., editors. Cenozoic paleogeography of the western United States. Pacific Section, Society of Economic Paleontologists and Mineralogists, Los Angeles, California, USA.

Dickinson, W.R. 1991. Tectonic setting of faulted Tertiary strata associated with the Catalina core complex in southern Arizona. Special Paper 264. Geological Society of America, Boulder, Colorado, USA.

Dickinson, W.R., and T.F. Lawton. 2001. Tectonic setting and sandstone petrofacies of the Bisbee Basin (USA-Mexico). Journal of South American Earth Sciences 14: 474-504.

Dickinson, W. R., A. R. Fiorillo, D. L. Hall, R. Monreal, A. R. Potochnik, and P. N. Swift. 1989. Cretaceous strata in southern Arizona. Pages 447-461 in P. Jenny and S.J. Reynolds, editors. Geologic evolution of Arizona. Digest 17. Arizona Geological Society, Tucson, Arizona, USA.

Dickinson, W.R., M.A. Klute, and W.L. Bilodeau. 1987. Tectonic setting and sedimentological features of Upper Mesozoic strata in southeastern Arizona. Special Paper 5. Arizona Bureau of Geology and Mineral Technology, Tucson, Arizona, USA.

Drewes, H. 1980. Tectonic map of southeast Arizona. 1980.. U.S. Geological Survey Miscellaneous Investigations Series Map I-1109 (scale 1:125,000).

Drewes, H. 1981. Geologic map and sections of the Bowie Mountain South quadrangle, Cochise County, Arizona. U.S. Geological Survey Miscellaneous Investigations Series Map I-1363 (scale 1:24,000).

Drewes, H. 1982. Geologic map and sections of the Cochise Head quadrangle and adjacent areas, Southeastern Arizona. U.S. Geological Survey Miscellaneous Investigations Series Map I-1312 (scale 1:24,000).

Dubiel, R.F. 1994. Triassic deposystems, paleogeography, and paleoclimate of the Western Interior. Pages 133-168 in M.V. Caputo, J.A. Peterson, and K.J. Franczyk, editors. Mesozoic systems of the Rocky Mountain region, USA. Rocky Mountain Section, Society for Sedimentary Geology, Denver, Colorado, USA.

Elder, W.P., and J.I. Kirkland. 1994. Cretaceous paleogeography of the southern Western Interior Region. Pages 415-440 in M.V. Caputo, J.A. Peterson, and K.J. Franczyk, editors. Mesozoic systems of the Rocky Mountain region, USA. Rocky Mountain Section, Society for Sedimentary Geology, Denver, Colorado, USA.

Gettings, M.E., and B.B. Houser. 2000. Depth to bedrock in the Upper San Pedro Valley, Cochise County, southeastern Arizona. Open-File Report 00-138. U.S. Geological Survey. Reston, Virginia, USA. (http://pubs.usgs.gov/of/2000/of00-138). Accessed 9 June 2010.

Graham, J. 2009. Chiricahua National Monument Geologic Resources Inventory Report. Natural Resource Report NPS/NRPC/GRD/NRR—2009/081. National Park Service, Denver, Colorado, USA. (http://www.nature.nps.gov/geology/inventory/gre_publications.cfm). Accessed 15 August 2011.

Graham, J. 2010. Saguaro National Park: geologic resources inventory report. Natural Resource Report NPS/NRPC/GRD/NRR—2010/233. National Park Service, Ft. Collins, Colorado, USA. (http://www.nature.nps.gov/geology/inventory/gre_publications.cfm). Accessed 15 August 2011.

Graham, J. 2011a. Tumacácori National Historical Park geologic resources inventory report. Natural Resource Report NPS/NRPC/GRD/NRR—2011/439. National Park Service, Fort Collins, Colorado, USA. (http://www.nature.nps.gov/geology/inventory/gre_publications.cfm). Accessed 16 September 2011.

Graham, J. 2011b. Fort Bowie National Historic Site: geologic resources inventory report. Natural Resource Report NPS/NRPC/GRD/NRR—2011/443. National Park Service, Ft. Collins, Colorado, USA. (http://www.nature.nps.gov/geology/inventory/gre_publications.cfm). Accessed 31 October 2011.

Haenggi, W.T., and W.R. Muehlberger. 2005. Chihuahua Trough; a Jurassic pull-apart basin. Special Paper – 393. Geological Society of America, Boulder, Colorado, USA.

Hall, K. A. 2010. Flood repairs finally completed. InsideNPS Headlines. April 20, 2010. http://inside.nps.gov/index.cfm?handler=viewincidentsarticle&type=Incidents&id=5026. Accessed 20 April 2010.

Hayes, M.J. 1988. Sedimentologic and tectonic history of the Late Cretaceous Fort Crittenden Formation in southeastern Arizona. Geologic Society of America Abstracts with Programs 20: 168.

Hayes, M.J. 1987. Depositional history of Upper Cretaceous Fort Crittenden Formation in southeastern Arizona. Pages 315-325 *in* W.R. Dickinson and M.A. Klute. Mesozoic rocks of southern Arizona and adjacent areas. Digest 18. Arizona Geological Society, Tucson, Arizona, USA.

Hayes, P.T. 1970. Mesozoic stratigraphy of the Mule and Huachuca Mountains, Arizona. Professional Paper 658-A. U. S. Geological Survey, Reston, Virginia, USA.

Hayes, P.T. and R.B. Raup. 1968. Geologic map of the Huachuca and Mustang Mountains southeastern Arizona. U.S. Geological Survey Miscellaneous Investigations Series Map I-509 (scale 1;48,000).

Hoffman, P.F. 1989. Precambrian geology and tectonic history of North America. Pages 447-512 *in* A.W. Bally and A.R. Palmer, editors. The geology of North America: An overview. The Geology of North America-A. Geological Society of America, Boulder, Colorado, USA.

Hon, K.A. and P. Lipman. 1994. Jurassic calderas in southeastern Arizona – the surface manifestation of a composite batholith. Circular C 1103-A. U. S. Geological Survey, Reston, Virginia, USA.

Hon, K.A., F. Gray, K.S. Bolm, K.A. Dempsey, and P.A. Pearthree. 2007. A digital geologic map of the Miller Peak, Nicksville, Bob Thompson Peak, and Montezuma Pass Quadrangles, Arizona. U.S. Geological Survey Scientific Investigations Map, SIM unpublished (scale 1:24,000).

Houk, R. 1999. Coronado National Memorial. Southwest Parks and Monuments Association, Tucson, Arizona, USA.

Karl, T.R., J.M. Melillo, and T.C. Peterson, editors. 2009. Global climate change impacts in the United States. Cambridge University Press. (http://www.globalchange.gov/publications/reports/sc ientific-assessments/us-impacts). Access June 12, 2010.

Kauffman, E. G. 1977. Geological and biological overview: Western Interior Cretaceous basin. Mountain Geologist 14: 75-99.

Kluth, C.F. 1983. Geology of the northern Canelo Hills and implications for the Mesozoic tectonics of southeastern Arizona. Pages 159-171 *in* M.W. Reynolds and E.D. Dolly, editors. Mesozoic paleogeography of west-central United States. Rocky Mountain Section, Society of Economic Paleontologists and Mineralogists, Denver, Colorado, USA.

Kring, D.A. 2002. Desert heat – volcanic fire: The geologic history of the Tucson Mountains and southern Arizona. Digest 21. Arizona Geological Society, Tucson, Arizona, USA.

Lawton, T.F. 1994. Tectonic setting of Mesozoic sedimentary basins, Rocky Mountain region, United States. Pages 1-26 *in* M.V. Caputo, J.A. Peterson, and K.J. Franczyk, editors. Mesozoic systems of the Rocky Mountain region, USA. Rocky Mountain Section, Society for Sedimentary Geology, Denver, Colorado, USA.

Lillie, R.J. 2005. Parks and plates: The geology of our national parks, monuments, and seashores. W.W. Norton and Company, New York, New York, USA.

Lipman, P.W. and J.T. Hagstrum. 1992. Jurassic ash-flow sheets, calderas, and related intrusions of the Cordilleran volcanic arc in southeastern Arizona: Implications for regional tectonics and ore deposits. Geological Society of America Bulletin 104: 32-39.

Menges, C.M. and P.A. Pearthree. 1989. Late Cenozoic tectonism in Arizona and its impact on regional landscape evolution. Pages 649-680 *in* P. Jenny and S.J. Reynolds, editors. Geologic evolution of Arizona. Digest 17. Arizona Geological Society, Tucson, Arizona, USA.

Mindat.org. n. d. State of Texas Mine, Montezuma Canyon, Hartford District (Huachuca Mountains District), Huachuca Mts, Cochise Co., Arizona, USA. Webpage. (http://www.mindat.org/loc-32764.html). Accessed February 1, 2010.

Morris, T.H., V.W. Manning, and S.M. Ritter. 2000. Geology of Capitol Reef National Park, Utah. Pages 85-106 *in* D.A. Sprinkel, T.C. Chidsey, Jr., and P.B. Anderson, editors. Geology of Utah's parks and monuments. Publication 28. Utah Geological Association, Salt Lake City, Utah, USA.

Morrison, R.B. 1991. Quaternary geology of the southern Basin and Range province. Pages 353-373 *in* R.B. Morrison, editor. Quaternary nonglacial geology: Conterminous U.S. The Geology of North America, K-2. Geological Society of America, Boulder, Colorado, USA.

National Park Service. 2006a. Geologic Resource Evaluation Scoping Summary, Coronado National Memorial, Arizona. National Park Service, Geologic Resources Division, Lakewood, CO. (http://www.nature.nps.gov/geology/inventory/ gre_publications.cfm#C). Accessed January 18, 2010.

National Park Service 2006b. Distrubed Lands. Webpage. Coronado National Memorial, Hereford, AZ. (http://www.nps.gov/coro/naturescience/ disturbedlands.htm). Accessed January 14, 2010.

National Park Service. 2007a. Stories. Webpage. Coronado National Memorial, Hereford, AZ. (http://www.nps.gov/coro/historyculture/stories.htm). Accessed January 14, 2010.

National Park Service. 2007b. Environmental assessment: Install bat-accessible gates at Crest Trail Mines, Coronado National Memorial, Cochise County, Arizona. Hereford, AZ: Coronado National Memorial. (http://www.nps.gov/coro/parkmgmt/upload/Coronado%20NMem%20Bat%20Gate%20EA%205-9-07.pdf). Accessed January 18, 2010.

National Park Service. 2008a. Permits. Webpage. Coronado National Memorial, Hereford, AZ. (http://www.nps.gov/coro/planyourvisit/permits.htm). Accessed April 28, 2010.

National Park Service. 2008b. Cave/Karst Systems. Webpage. Coronado National Memorial, Hereford, AZ. (http://www.nps.gov/coro/naturescience/cave.htm). Accessed April 28, 2010.

National Park Service. n. d. Coronado Cave. Webpage. Coronado National Memorial, Hereford, AZ. (http://www.nps.gov/archive/coro/cave.htm). Accessed February 1, 2010.

Nations, D., J.C. Wilt, and R.H. Hevly. 1985. Cenozoic paleogeography of Arizona. Pages 335-356 in R.M. Flores and S.S. Kaplan, editors. Cenozoic paleogeography of west-central United States. Rocky Mountain Section, Society of Economic Paleontologists and Mineralogists, Denver, Colorado, USA.

Oldow, J S., A.W. Bally, H.G. Avé Lallemant, and W.P. Leeman. 1989. Phanerozoic evolution of the North American Cordillera; United States and Canada. Pages 139-232 in A.W. Bally and A.R. Palmer, editors. The geology of North America: An overview. The Geology of North America-A, Geological Society of America, Boulder, Colorado, USA.

Pallister, J.S., E.A. du Bray, and D.B. Hall. 1997. Guide to the volcanic geology of Chiricahua National Monument and vicinity, Cochise County, Arizona. Pamphlet to accompany the U.S. Geological Survey Miscellaneous Investigations Series Map I-2541.

Pearthree P.A. and A. Youberg. 2006. Recent debris flows and floods in southern Arizona. Arizona Geology 36: 1-6.

Peterson, F. 1994. Sand dunes, sabkhas, streams, and shallow seas: Jurassic paleogeography in the southern part of the Western Interior Basin. Pages 233-272 in M.V. Caputo, J.A. Peterson, and K.J. Franczyk, editors. Mesozoic systems of the Rocky Mountain region, USA. Rocky Mountain Section, Society for Sedimentary Geology, Denver, Colorado, USA.

Peterson, J.A. 1980. Permian paleogeography and sedimentary provinces, west central United States. Pages 271-292 in T.D. Fouch and E.R. Magathan, editors. Paleozoic paleogeography of west-central United States. Rocky Mountain Section, Society of Economic Paleontologists and Mineralogists, Denver, Colorado, USA.

Raup, D.M. 1991. Extinction: Bad Genes or Bad Luck? W.W. Norton and Company, New York, New York, USA.

Santucci, V.L., J.P. Kenworthy, and A.L. Mims. 2009. Monitoring in situ paleontological resources. Pages 189–204 in R. Young and L. Norby, editors. Geological Monitoring. Geological Society of America, Boulder, Colorado, USA. (http://nature.nps.gov/geology/monitoring/paleo.cfm). Accessed August 18, 2011).

Spencer, J.E. and S.J. Reynolds. 1989. Middle Tertiary tectonics of Arizona and adjacent areas. Pages 539-574 in P. Jenny and S.J. Reynolds, editors. Geologic evolution of Arizona. Digest 17. Arizona Geological Society, Tucson, Arizona, USA.

Stevens, C.H., P. Stone, and J.S. Miller. 2005. A new reconstruction of the Paleozoic continental margin of southwestern North America; implications for the nature and timing of continental truncation and the possible role of the Mojave-Sonora megashear. Special Paper – 393. Geological Society of America, Boulder, Colorado, USA.

Sumner, J.R. 1977. The Sonora earthquake of 1887. Bulletin of the Seismological Society of America 67: 1219-1223.

Toomey, R.S. III. 2009. Geological monitoring of caves and associated landscapes. Pages 27-46 in R. Young and L. Norby, editors. Geological monitoring. Geological Society of America, Boulder, Colorado, USA. (http://nature.nps.gov/geology/monitoring/cavekarst.cfm). Accessed August 18, 2011.

Tosdal, R.M., G.B. Haxel, and J.E. Wright. 1989. Jurassic geology of the Sonoran Desert region, southern Arizona, southeastern California, and northernmost Sonora: Construction of a continental-margin magmatic arc. Pages 397-434 in P. Jenny and S.J. Reynolds, editors. Geologic evolution of Arizona. Digest 17. Arizona Geological Society, Tucson, Arizona, USA.

Tuftin, S.E. and R.C. Armstrong. 1994. Mineral appraisal of the Coronado National Forest Part 8: Huachuca Mountains Unit, Cochise and Santa Cruz Counties, Arizona. Mineral Land Assessment Open-File report MLA 1-94. Department of the Interior, Washington, D.C., USA.

Tweet, J.S., V.L. Santucci, and J.P. Kenworthy. 2008. Paleontological resource inventory and monitoring Sonoran Desert Network. Natural Resource Technical Report NPS/NRPC/NRTR 2008/130. National Park Service, Natural Resource Program Center, Fort Collins, Colorado, USA.

U.S. Geological Survey. 2009. Arizona Earthquake History. U.S. Geological Survey, Earthquake Hazards Program, Reston, VA. Webpage. (http://earthquake.usgs.gov/earthquakes/states/arizona/history.php). Accessed February 2, 2010.

U.S. Geological Survey. 2010. Stream flow measurements for Arizona. Station USGS 09470500 San Pedro River and Palominas, AZ. (http://waterdata.usgs.gov/az/nwis/measurements/?site_no=09470500&amp). Accessed May 31, 2010.

Water Resources Division. 2000. Baseline water quality data inventory and analysis: Coronado National Memorial. Water Resources Division Technical Report NPS/NRWRD/NRTR-99/234 (August 2000). Fort Collins, Colorado, USA. (http://www.nature.nps.gov/water/horizon.cfm). Accessed January 18, 2010.

Webb, R.H., C.S. Magirl, P.G. Griffiths, and D.E. Boyer. 2008. Debris flows and floods in southeastern Arizona from extreme precipitation in July 2006 – magnitude, frequency, and sediment delivery. Open-File Report 2008-1274. U. S. Geological Survey, Reston, Virginia, USA.

Wieczorek, T.G.F., and J.B. Snyder. 2009. Monitoring slope movements. Pages 245–271 in R. Young and L. Norby, editors. Geological Monitoring. Geological Society of America, Boulder, Colorado, USA. (http://nature.nps.gov/geology/monitoring/slopes.cfm). Accessed August 18, 2011.

Wohl, E.E. and P.A. Pearthree. 1991. Debris flows as geomorphic agents in the Huachuca Mountains of southeastern Arizona. Geomorphology 4: 273-292.

Youberg, A., M.L. Cline, J.P. Cook, P.A. Pearthree, and R.H. Webb. 2008. Geologic mapping of debris flow deposits in the Santa Catalina Mountains, Pima County, Arizona. Arizona Geological Survey Digital Map DM-DF-01. (http://repository.azgs.az.gov/uri_gin/azgs/dlio/118). Accessed 8 March 2011.

Additional References

This section lists additional references, resources, and web sites that may be of use to resource managers. Web addresses are current as of August 2011.

Geology of National Park Service Areas

National Park Service Geologic Resources Division (Lakewood, Colorado). http://nature.nps.gov/geology/

NPS Geologic Resources Inventory. http://www.nature.nps.gov/geology/inventory/gre_publications.cfm

Harris, A. G., E. Tuttle, and S. D. Tuttle. 2003. Geology of National Parks. Sixth Edition. Kendall/Hunt Publishing Co., Dubuque, Iowa, USA.

Kiver, E. F. and D. V. Harris. 1999. Geology of U.S. parklands. John Wiley and Sons, Inc., New York, New York, USA.

Lillie, R. J. 2005. Parks and Plates: The geology of our national parks, monuments, and seashores. W.W. Norton and Co., New York, New York, USA. [Geared for interpreters].

NPS Geoscientist-in-the-parks (GIP) internship and guest scientist program. http://www.nature.nps.gov/geology/gip/index.cfm

Resource Management/Legislation Documents

NPS 2006 Management Policies (Chapter 4, Natural Resource Management): http://www.nps.gov/policy/mp/policies.html#_Toc157232681

NPS-75: Natural Resource Inventory and Monitoring Guideline: http://www.nature.nps.gov/nps75/nps75.pdf

NPS Natural Resource Management Reference Manual #77: http://www.nature.nps.gov/Rm77/

Geologic Monitoring Manual
R. Young and L. Norby, editors. Geological Monitoring. Geological Society of America, Boulder, Colorado. http://nature.nps.gov/geology/monitoring/index.cfm

NPS Technical Information Center (Denver, repository for technical (TIC) documents): http://etic.nps.gov/

Geological Survey Websites

Arizona Geological Survey: http://www.azgs.state.az.us/

U.S. Geological Survey: http://www.usgs.gov/

Geological Society of America: http://www.geosociety.org/

American Geological Institute: http://www.agiweb.org/

Association of American State Geologists: http://www.stategeologists.org/

Other Geology/Resource Management Tools

Bates, R. L. and J. A. Jackson, editors. American Geological Institute dictionary of geological terms (3rd Edition). Bantam Doubleday Dell Publishing Group, New York.

U.S. Geological Survey National Geologic Map Database (NGMDB): http://ngmdb.usgs.gov/

U.S. Geological Survey Geologic Names Lexicon (GEOLEX; geologic unit nomenclature and summary): http://ngmdb.usgs.gov/Geolex/geolex_home.html

U.S. Geological Survey Geographic Names Information System (GNIS; search for place names and geographic features, and plot them on topographic maps or aerial photos): http://gnis.usgs.gov/

U.S. Geological Survey GeoPDFs (download searchable PDFs of any topographic map in the United States): http://store.usgs.gov (click on "Map Locator").

U.S. Geological Survey Publications Warehouse (many USGS publications are available online): http://pubs.er.usgs.gov

U.S. Geological Survey, description of physiographic provinces: http://tapestry.usgs.gov/Default.html

Appendix: Scoping Session Participants

The following is a list of participants from the GRI scoping session for Coronado National Memorial, held on April 6, 2006. The contact information and email addresses in this appendix may be outdated; please contact the Geologic Resources Division for current information. The scoping meeting summary was used as the foundation for this GRI report. The original scoping summary document is available on the GRI publications web site: http://www.nature.nps.gov/geology/inventory/ gre_publications.cfm.

Name	Position	Affiliation	Phone	E-mail
Covington, Sid	Geologist	NPS Geologic Resources Division	303-969-2154	sid_covington@nps.gov
Daly, Maggi	Visitor Use Assistant	NPS Coronado National Memorial	520-366-5515	magi_daly@nps.gov
Ferguson, Charles	Geologist	Arizona Geological Survey (AZGS)	520-770-3500	ferguson@geo.arizona.edu
Graham, John	Geologist	Colorado State University		
Gray, Floyd	Geologist	U.S. Geological Survey	520-670-5582	fgray@usgs.gov
Hall, Kym	Superintendent	NPS Coronado National Memorial	520-366-5515 ext. 21	kym_hall@nps.gov
Kerbo, Ron	Cave specialist	NPS Geologic Resources Division	303-969-2097	Ron_Kerbo@nps.gov
LaCroix, Kelly	Graduate Student	University of Arizona		
O'Meara, Stephanie	Geologist	Colorado State University	970-225-3584	Stephanie_O'Meara@ partner.nps.gov
Torres, Frank	Chief of Interpretation	NPS Coronado National Memorial	520-366-5515	frank_torres@nps.gov
Covington, Sid	Geologist	NPS Geologic Resources Division	303-969-2154	sid_covington@nps.gov
Daly, Maggi	Visitor Use Assistant	NPS Coronado National Memorial	520-366-5515	magi_daly@nps.gov

The Department of the Interior protects and manages the nation's natural resources and cultural heritage; provides scientific and other information about those resources; and honors its special responsibilities to American Indians, Alaska Natives, and affiliated Island Communities.

NPS 401/109347, August 2011